COMPA$$IONATE CAPITALI$M

The Intersection of Economic Growth and Social Justice

"Freedom consists not in doing what we want, but in having the
right to do what we ought."
-*Pope St. John Paul II*

Gerard L. Hasenhuettl

Compassionate Capitalism
Copyright © 2017 Gerard L. Hasenhuettl
Cheetahtech International, LLC
Port Saint Lucie, FL
ISBN 978-0-9986953-5-8
Library of Congress Control Number: 2017948797

Cover design by Jennifer Richardson and Janet Sierzant
Cover art by Velia Sebald

The Lotus Flower is a recognized symbol of compassion.

La Maison Publishing, Inc.
Vero Beach Florida
The Hibiscus City
lamaisonpublishing@gmail.com

Dedicated to Mothers and Teachers who have been shortchanged by the law of supply and demand.

Also dedicated to Anthony Sebald, a man who had a brilliant mind and a compassionate heart.

PREFACE

Compassionate and capitalism are two words that may have never been used in the same sentence, let alone as modifier and noun. Of course, the history of capitalism evokes very few accounts of compassionate actions. My objective while researching and writing this book was not to convince anyone that capitalism, by its nature, is compassionate. Rather, it is to ask the question whether it is possible to create such a system, and how it could be done.

History professors have always told us that we need to learn from the mistakes of our history so we don't repeat them. So with that attitude, I began in Part I to examine how humanity dealt with survival, wealth, poverty, and business. In the earliest days of humanity, there was probably no driving force to join people together in communities. There were plenty of game and edible plants to assist survival. As the population increased, there was likely a period where the strong dominated the weak. Since we only know about these early days from the fossil record and artifacts from archeologists, there is little information how humans set the rules. When humans began to draw pictures and write, history began to take shape. There would have been many unexplained phenomena in their environment, like lightning, wild animals, wildfires, or earthquakes. In many cases, they turned to God (or gods) for protection. Their codes were believed to have come from God.

The economic history of the world is essentially the history of innovation. Inventors were nameless, leaving us to wonder who learned to control fire, invented the wheel, or thought to heat copper ore in a fire. Initially, economic activity consisted of hunting and gathering. As more innovations emerged, laws were established to deal with them.

In Part II, we explore the topic of comparative political economy. Early economic systems were command economies controlled by kings, warlords, or their designees. Through history, a number of systems were tried, including communism, capitalism, socialism, fascism, and blended aspects. In communism, wealth is distributed equally, but innovation and economic growth are difficult. In capitalism, innovation and growth can flourish, but wealth is unequally distributed.

Part III proposes a new traditional economy which is based on economic and personal freedom, equal opportunity for development, and a priority for the involuntary poor. Compliance would be voluntary, but subject to the reality of social media. The roles of individuals, companies, governments, and the faith community are elaborated. This new traditional economy is called Compassionate Capitalism.

Part IV describes the serendipity that some are already practicing this new traditional economy. Substantial social movements have been spawned by the dedication of a single individual. Some companies have implemented a one-for-one (one unit value to the poor for every unit sold) into their business plan. The problem of continuity of programs for the poor in public companies is recognized, and strategies to deal with it are proposed.

Appendices which summarize the Manifesto for Compassionate Capitalism and parallels of natural laws with economic laws and behavior are included.

Political partisans on polar extremes will have criticisms of the proposals for this new traditional economy. All I ask is for a fair examination of the evidence, followed by proposals for improvements.

Even if Compassionate Capitalism is not politically accepted, I am certain that individuals and companies will continue to practice it on a community level.

Gerard L. Hasenhuettl

ACKNOWLEDGEMENTS

The author is indebted to Professor Charles Bennet of Gannon University who mapped the tortuous path through the literature in the field of political economy. Valuable assistance was contributed by Yael Herbsmann of the Judaic Library at the University of Florida and Elaine Sabol at Indian River State College to access the voluminous quantity of literature. I am grateful to Shirley Moore and Julia Hasenhuettl who assisted in preparation and proofreading of the manuscript.

Stephanie Basile is thanked for a superb job of professional editing. Helpful suggestions were provided by Tom and Mary Lyons and Edward Sharrer.

Table of Contents

Figures

Tables

PART I

SEARCHING FOR JUSTICE

The human race started out very simply, hunting for food, warmth, shelter, and an attractive mate. As humanity developed, it became obvious, that if people were going to live together in harmony, rules and traditions would need to be created. The first chapter explores concepts of right and wrong, and then proposes broad principles of social and economic justice. Chapter 2 explores the codes for business conduct by major religious traditions. Chapter 3 summarizes the history of economic activity, and the innovations that drove progress.

Chapter 1

Good vs. Evil: A Legal and Ethical Framework

*"I believe in a higher power and I believe in
good and bad, right and wrong."*
-Leif Garrett-

*"Are right and wrong convertible terms,
dependent on popular opinion?"*
-William Lloyd Garrison-

*"Our world is at the crossroads.
We have a choice, right and wrong."*
-LLCoolJ-

1.1 Introduction

In order to decide which is the best economic system (assuming there is only one), we must examine the history of human interactions and the evolution of laws and morals. In ancient times one can imagine a hunter bartering his game with a farmer or a weaver. One can also imagine the strong taking advantage of the

Gerard L. Hasenhuettl

weak and battling with others who are strong, for possessions or mates. In a hostile ancient world, men needed to cooperate with one another in order to survive. Perhaps they decided that the best way to deal with a saber-toothed tiger was to gang up on him, and have him for dinner. Laws were then needed to maintain the functionality of the tribe. Of course, history is replete with tribal warfare, even recently. Victorious tribes would impose their laws on the vanquished.

The ultimate source of law is a subject hotly debated to this day. Were laws dictated by God to rescue His highest creation from self-destruction? Or, did man realize on his own that a code was required to preserve his species, or at least his tribe? Was the Golden Rule the inspired word of God? Or, did the tribe realize that stealing another's goods, or mate, were wrong because every person would object to the same treatment?

Thomas Sowell has postulated that social political and economic disagreements are caused by a clash of visions, which he defines as pre-cognitive thought[1]. For simplicity, he categorizes visions as "constrained" or "unconstrained". An individual espousing a constrained vision holds that man intends to act for the benefit of the common good. Condorcet, Freud, Godwin, and Rousseau expressed aspects of this vision. In his recent book, *Culture Warrior*, Bill O'Reilly divides the population into two groups[2]: Traditionalists and Secular Progressives (I prefer the term "Rational Humanists.") Traditionalists believe in traditional values, e.g. God, country, and marriage between a man and a woman. O'Reilly's traditionalists resemble Sowell's definition of constrained visionaries. Secular progressives challenge these beliefs and think that the world may be greatly improved. Note the

---

[1] T. Sowell, *A Conflict of Visions: Ideological Orgins of Political Struggles.* (Basic Books, 2002).
[2] W. O'Reilly, *Culture Warrior* (New York: Broadway Books, 2006).

2

similarity to unconstrained vision. Their implement for determining the best process is articulated rationality from the most enlightened individuals. The debate between the two visions can be quite vociferous, as the current era of political polarization attests. Progressives give little or no weight to traditional values, because they may be outdated, and therefore not applicable in the current social environment. Traditionalists believe it presumptuous that any individual or group can be the repository of all human knowledge. They prefer to rely on the collective experience of all preceding generations. They also warn that articulated rationality can easily slide into rationalization of evil, justified by the search for a more perfect society (i.e. the end justifies the means).

As with other classifications, Sowell admits that these groups are not monoliths. However, the aggregate political views of these groups often influence or determine an economic system. Traditionalists tend to be capitalists, while secular progressives may lean more toward socialism.

Of course, requiring everyone in the human race to be pigeonholed into only two visions is an obvious oversimplification. Libertarians tend to be economic conservatives but socially liberal. President George W. Bush popularized the term "Compassionate Conservative," apparently the mirror image of the libertarian viewpoint. Individuals working together for a cause may have opposing points of view on other issues. Charismatic pastor Rick Warren has expressed his willingness to work with feminist groups to fight prostitution and pornography, but strongly opposes their positions on abortion. This pragmatic view may be summarized as: "Let's work together on problems where we agree and reject the accusations of guilt by association."

Gerard L. Hasenhuettl

Visions of individuals, groups, or whole societies are also dynamic. They may evolve slowly, or undergo a sudden, traumatic "road to Damascus" conversion[3]. I have personally experienced the latter phenomenon. Originally pro-choice, I was watching a medical training film of an abortion, and was immediately overwhelmed by the reality that this was wrong. The experience was a turning point in my career and worldview. Gradual changes may melt away one vision and build another so slowly that an inflection point may be imperceptible.

Since we are seeking definitions for right and wrong, good and evil, we must explore the philosophies of the two visions. Traditionalists believe in the collective wisdom that billions of humans have formed in the past. They believe in sharp boundaries between right and wrong. In the United States, Judeo-Christian values are their guide post. Progressives believe in the intellect and reason to define their beliefs. Distinctions between right and wrong are viewed as complex analyses. What is wrong in one set of circumstances may be acceptable in another. Enormous weight is given to the end result. In this vision, the end is often used to justify the means. Extreme examples of this include the mass exterminations in the French, Russian, Chinese, and Cambodian revolutions. These casualties were treated as mere process costs in pursuit of a perfect society (you can't make an omelet without breaking some eggs). Rationality had given way to rationalization. However, reactionary traditionalist regimes have also committed such atrocities. The holocaust in Nazi Germany and the death squads in Latin America are vivid illustrations.

So, with such an enormous chasm between visions, how do we get to an agreement on what is right and what is wrong? Pope St. John Paul II, a highly regarded traditionalist, may have given us a starting point. "How do I distinguish good from evil? The answer

---

[3] T. Sowell, p. 99.

is only possible thanks to the splendor of truth which shines forth deep within the human spirit[4]." Traditionalists would say that this vision originated from the Tree of Knowledge in the Garden of Eden, and has been refined through each succeeding generation. Sociopath's aside, all individuals have some sense of right and wrong. But how does a zero-based free thinker arrive at what is right and wrong, just and unjust? Not surprisingly, there are a multitude of rationalist theories. Progressives, however, are very sensitive detectors for cases of hypocrisy and injustice, where the circumstances run counter to reason and logic. The "angry left" has probably attained that reputation because of that sensitivity. Justice, however, seems much harder to define. Is it merely the absence of injustice?

1.2 A Step Toward Agreement

How do we start to build consensus on definitions? One way is the previous example set by Rick Warren. Let's apply this to another situation. One group sincerely believes that greenhouse gases, generated by fossil fuels, produce destructive changes in the earth's climate. The other group rejects this, but believes that imported oil poses a threat to national security. One solution that ameliorates both problems is conservation. However, as in most conflicts, there is still disagreement. The first group believes this approach should be mandated, using methods such as rationing or limits on consumer purchasing decisions. The second group believes in individual freedom and believes that purchasing decisions should be market driven. A compromise to this conflict has already been achieved. The government sets fleet standards for auto manufacturers, while the consumer is free to buy whatever they want. Recent history is showing that as gas prices increase, so does the demand for fuel-efficient vehicles. However,

---

[4] Pope John Paul II, Papal Encyclical, *Veritatis Splendor*, Vatican Press (1993)

this is an uneasy truce, as both sides fight over next steps. Thomas and Beckel have suggested that most individuals holding polarized positions can agree on at least some ideas (common ground)[5]. In the first twenty-two chapters, they recount a contemporary history of political polarization in the United States. Four Chapters propose ways to arrive at common ground. Their five-point program is: 1) Both sides admit there is a problem; 2) A solution should be developed, which includes orthodoxy from both sides; 3) Innovative approaches should be incorporated; 4) Political cover should be sought from respected third parties; and, 5) Deep animosity on unrelated issues should be avoided during the process.

Beckel and Thomas predicted that the wave elections of 2006 and 2008 would marginalize polarizers in the U.S. political system. Indeed, Barack Obama was elected on a promise to change the tone in Washington. Unfortunately, the Democrats forced through an unpopular healthcare reform bill on a straight partisan line vote, and some questionable parliamentary tactics. This gave birth to the Tea Party, which exacted its revenge in the midterm election of 2010. Another dissonant note was that the voters rejected Senator John McCain, who had a solid record of finding common ground. (Remember the McCain-Feingold and McCain-Kennedy bills.) Nevertheless, we can hope that eventually, the atmosphere will become less toxic allowing for more common ground to be exposed.

Some contemporary issues could be solved with a "Common Ground" approach. The 2007 McCain-Kennedy bill appeared to have the first two guidelines for resolution. Border security, a path to legal status, and a crackdown on lawbreaking employers were

---

[5] C. Thomas, , Beckel,,R., *Common Ground: How to Stop the Partisan War That Is Destroying America* (New York N.Y.: Harper Collins Publishers, 2007).

all in it. I believe this measure failed due to an absence of trust between the parties. An innovative twist (#3) may have saved it. Quantitative measures for the success of each element could have been established, e.g. height of a fence, how many border agents, etc. The elements would have then been linked. For example, for every 100 miles of border fence constructed, one million immigrants would be processed. An independent monitoring group (#4) could have kept score. Any attempts at bad faith would have been transparent to the public. With the concept of common ground, let's explore definitions of right and wrong that might be accepted by a large majority.

1.3 Social and Economic Justice

A fair amount has been published concerning social justice and economic justice, often from the same viewpoint. Thomas Aquinas discussed distributive justice, a rough equivalent of economic justice. I will be very presumptuous and develop two separate constructs. In some areas they will agree, while in others, they will conflict.

A possible starting point for social justice is the United Nations Declaration of Human Rights (see Table 1.1)[6]. It was most likely derived by a combination of tradition and rational thought. The preamble asserts a common understanding of rights and freedoms, and asserts that adherence to them will promote peace among nations. All men and women are deemed to be free, equal, and deserving of dignity (Articles 1 and 2). Everyone has the right to life, liberty, and security of person (Articles 3-5). All are entitled to equal protection before the law (Articles 6 and 7). Articles 8-12

---

[6] United Nations, *The Universal Declaration of Human Rights*, http//:www.un.org/en/documents/udhr/index.shtml.

specify individual rights under national and international laws. Everyone is assured of the right to travel and freely choose their own nationality (Articles 13-15). This right may appear to conflict with the right of individual nations to secure their own borders. Article 16 defines protection of marriage and the family unit. The right to own property, individually or in common, is asserted in Articles 17. Articles 18-21 establish freedom of religion and thought and the right to participate in government. Article 22 broadly states that each individual has the freedom to seek personal development. Subsequent articles (23-24, 26, and 27) specify the rights of workers and the right to education. A right to the necessary elements of a standard of living, such as food, clothing, shelter and access to medical care is defined (Article 25). In return for these rights and freedoms, individuals have responsibilities to their governments, communities, and the rights of others (Articles 29 and 30).

The U.N. portrait is a collection of individuals who are equally free and have responsibilities to respect one another. Even within this ideal construct, there are conflicting principles. There is a right to work and to own property. But governments must collect taxes in order to provide for the common good. What are the limits of governmental power? Should individuals be permitted to pass their property to their heirs? Such thorny questions are the stuff of intense political debate. The overarching principles are often overlooked in battles over these conflicts.

Table 1.1 U. N. Declarations of Human Rights

Article 1	All human beings are born free and equal in dignity and rights.
Article 2	Everyone is entitled to all the rights & freedoms set forth in this Declaration, without distinction of any kind.
Article 3	Everyone has the right to life, liberty, and security of person.
Article 4	No one shall be held in slavery or servitude: slavery and the slave trade shall be prohibited in all their forms.
Article 5	No one shall be subjected to torture or to cruel, inhuman or degrading treatment or punishment.
Article 6	Everyone has the right to recognition everywhere as a person before the law.
Article 7	All are equal before the law and are entitled without any discrimination to equal protection of the law.
Article 8	Everyone has the right to an effective remedy by the competent national tribunals.
Article 9	No right shall be subjected to arbitrary arrest, detention or exile.
Article 10	Everyone is entitled to a fair hearing before an independent and impartial tribunal.
Article 11.1	Everyone is entitled to the presumption of innocence until proven guilty.
Article 11.2	No one shall be held guilty of anything that is not a penal offense under national or international law.
Article 12	No one shall be deprived of his right to

	privacy, home, or correspondence.
Article 13.1	Everyone has freedom of movement within the boundaries of any state.
Article 13.2	Everyone has the right to leave his country and to return.
Article 14.1	Everyone has the right to seek asylum from persecution in another country.
Article 14.2	This right may not be invoked in a case of genuine prosecution for a non-political crime.
Article 15.1	Everyone has the right to a nationality.
Article 15.2	No one can be deprived of his nationality, nor the right to change his nationality.
Article 16.1	Men and women of full age have the right to marry, and to form a family.
Article 16.2	Marriage may be entered into only with the free and full consent of the spouses.
Article 16.3	The family is the fundamental and natural group of society.
Article 17.1	Everyone has the right to own property, alone or in association with others.
Article 17.2	No one shall be arbitrarily deprived of his property.
Article 18	Everyone has the right to free thought, conscience, and religion.
Article 19	Everyone has the freedom of opinion and expression.
Article 20.1	Everyone has the right of peaceful assembly and association.
Article 20.2	No one may be compelled to belong to

	an association.
Article 21.1	Everyone has the right to take part in the government of his country.
Article 21.2	Everyone has an equal right to public service in his country.
Article 21.3	The will of the people shall be the authority of government, which shall be expressed in periodic free and fair elections.
Article 22	Everyone has the right to social security based on the economic and social resources of his country.
Article 23.1	Everyone has the right to work, choice of employment, fair working conditions, and protection against unemployment.
Article 23.2	Everyone has the right to equal pay for equal work.
Article 23.3	Everyone who works has the right to equitable compensation.
Article 23.4	Everyone has the right to form and to join a trade union.
Article 24	Everyone has the right to leisure, including reasonable working hours and paid vacations.
Article 25.1	Everyone has the right to a standard of living adequate for himself and his family.
Article 25.2	Motherhood and childhood are entitled to special care and protection.
Article 26.1	Everyone is entitled to an education, which shall be free, at least at the primary level.
Article 26.2	Education shall be directed to the full

	development of the human personality and dignity.
Article 26.3	Parents have the prior right to choose the type of education given to their children.
Article 27.1	Every person has the right to fully participate in the cultural life of the community.
Article 27.2	Everyone is entitled to the protection of their intellectual property.
Article 28	Everyone is entitled to a social and international order in which he can enjoy the rights set forth in this Declaration.
Article 29.1	Everyone has a duty to the country in which he resides.
Article 29.2	Limitations on a person's exercise of his rights and freedoms are only subject to law.
Article 29.3	These rights and freedoms shall not be exercised for any cause contrary to the United Nations.
Article 30	Nothing in this Declaration may be interpreted to destroy any of the rights and freedoms set forth.

Rather than take the well-worn approach of extending social justice to define economic (distributive) justice, I will again be presumptuous and construct a system from commonly held beliefs. Here again, it is unclear whether the tenets descended from tradition or rational common sense.

1.3.1 Work and Compensation

For thousands of years, human beings have worked with and for one another. Excluding slavery and indentured servitude, the following commonly accepted beliefs about employer/employee relationships have developed:

1) Those who work hard deserve just compensation.
2) Individuals who risk their assets are entitled to reap rewards.
3) Those who perform work, which richly benefits society, should receive increased compensation.

If these first three principals were strictly enforced, the richest people in our society would be farmers, mothers, and teachers. Fortunately or unfortunately, these tenets have been overruled by the inflexible economic law of supply and demand. Unfortunately for the individuals, but fortunately for society, there is an abundance of people willing to assume these careers. Figure 1.1 shows a typical curve, which relates the price with the variables supply and demand.

How Supply and Demand Set Market Price

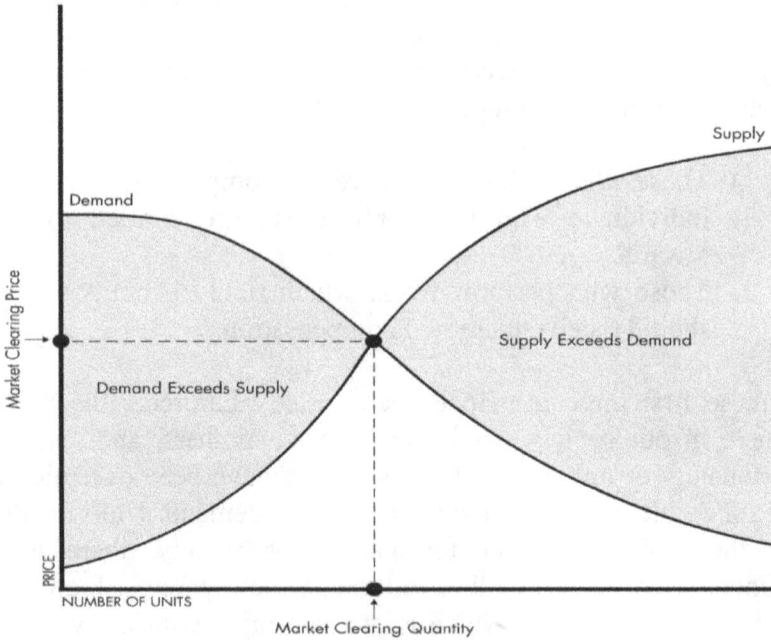

Fortunately, human beings are not an inanimate commodity and can differentiate themselves in a free market. For example, a chemistry teacher who has an advanced degree and is bilingual can command a higher value for his or her services:

4) Education and talent should be rewarded by higher salaries.
5) Those who achieve positive results should be rewarded monetarily.

Socialists may disagree on the last two points. Hahnel, for example, considers ability to be a result of a genetic lottery[7]. He would level the educational differences by publicly funding all education. On point 5, he would reward effort, rather than results. We will return to Hahnel's proposals for cooperative libertarian socialism in a later chapter. It should also be noted that a recent trend toward an entrepreneur economy may cause us to re-examine some of these beliefs.

1.3.2 Trade and Commerce

In the earliest economic transactions of the human race, goods and services were freely bartered between individuals. The earliest contracts were verbal agreements. As civilization developed, mankind discovered the efficiency of free markets. Hunters, farmers, and clothiers began to offer their wares in a central market. Peddlers, the earliest traveling salesmen, moved from town to town to market their products. Barter transactions became cumbersome, so systems of currency were introduced. Currencies were developed around precious metal and stones, which could be easily carried. However, in periods of financial distress, like the Great Depression, people returned to the barter system for day-to-day survival. Goods could be traded for other goods or necessary services. For example, a deli owner could provide meat to an electrician, who could repair the deli's wiring.

Human nature being what it is (remember the 5% rule), individuals began to take advantage of one another. Standards and codes of conduct had to be established to restore equity to the marketplace. Traditionalists claim these principles are based on religious teachings of morality and justice. In western markets, they can cite the Ten Commandments, the Talmud, and the

---

[7] R. Hahnel, *Economic Justice and Democracy: From Competition to Cooperation* (Routledge, 2005).

Golden Rule. Secular progressives will point to the existential threat to markets, posed by rampant unjust practices. Civil codes had to be created in order to preserve the integrity of the economy. Many of today's regulations are descendants of Roman law and the Code of Hammurabi. We can coalesce principles of just markets into a few basic points.

1.3.2.1 Products and Services

a) Products should be safe and designed for good quality. Producers must avoid compromising this principle in a drive to cut costs. Recent examples, such as lead paint on toys, defective drywall, and E. coli in ground meat, erode the confidence of consumers in the entire industry.

b) Products and services must be true to the claims that are made about them. For example, a drug that is acclaimed to cure cancer must be validated through experience. Weights and measures for all products must be accurate and disclosed to the consumer. Contracts should be written to accurately describe the service provided. Fine print and cryptic language should not be used to confuse the average person.

1.3.2.2 Competition and Pricing

a) In a competitive free market, all participants must be treated fairly to achieve economic justice.

b) Prices or products and services should be fair. In a free market economy, prices are determined by supply, demand, and the extent of competition. When prices are arbitrarily set too low, as in a command economy, shortages occur because marginal producers are unwilling to sell at a loss. Predatory pricing occurs when a strong firm prices below their cost to drive other firms out of the business. This may lead to monopoly status in the market.

c) Laws and rules governing competition must not favor or discriminate against any firm. Monopolies do not benefit society because they produce fewer units than firms in a competitive marketplace. Firms should not use political connections to gain an advantage over their competitors, e.g. "crony capitalism."

Armed with the foregoing principles of Social and Economic Justice, we will attempt to define an economic structure that is just, but provides the greatest potential for prosperity for the population. The next chapter will examine the influences of traditional values and articulated rationality on economic systems. In Part II, economic history and comparative economic systems will be examined. A rationale for Compassionate Capitalism will be advanced. Part III will describe elements of this system which are currently being practiced by organizations and individuals. In Part IV, strategies will be proposed for corporations, small businesses, and individuals to become involved. The costs and benefits will be frankly evaluated.

Chapter 2

Religious Tradition and Business Ethics

"Freely you have received, freely give."
-Matthew 10:8-

2.1 A Cultural Overview

In the previous chapter, we examined the polar positions of Traditionalist and Secularists. In the earliest societies, commerce was governed by strength. The strong conquered the weak and dictated terms of servitude. As societies recognized this as an unstable situation, laws concerning business ethics were promulgated, often by religious authorities. However, in the modern era economics has evolved into a secular, often highly mathematical science. In this chapter, we will explore the influence of religion and rational humanism on business ethics and economics.

Through history, scholars have questioned why some countries or regions of the world became wealthy, while others were mired in poverty. Landes has contributed a fairly comprehensive treatment of this subject[8]. He and others have suggested that religious differences played a prominent role. For example, Northern Europe was relatively wealthy, compared to the heavily Catholic South[9]. However, like all complex problems, there are a number of confounding variables. As Landes points out, nature itself is unfair[10]. Warm climates are exhausting places to work, have more pests and disease, and rain may be unpredictable. But, since religion has an influence on business ethics, we will examine it.

Virtually every religion has teachings that define how followers should interact in business situations. In many ancient civilizations, governments were theocracies and these teachings were codified into laws. Modern theocracies still adhere to at least a modified theocratic law. In countries with secular governments, laws governing business still contain underlying traditional principles. For example, laws in most Western countries are rooted in Judao-Christian ethics. In this chapter, we will attempt to capture the spirit of these teachings. A logical beginning would be to examine the three Middle Eastern traditions of Judaism, Christianity, and Islam. Rodney Wilson has written an excellent overview of these traditions and their teachings on economic matters[11] . Not surprisingly, there are many areas of agreement, and a few points of disagreement.

---

[8] D.S. Landes, *The Wealth and Poverty of Nations: Why Some Are So Rich and Some So Poor, W.W. Norton & Company, 1998.*

[9] a) Ibid., pp. 38, 139-40, 174-86, b) M. Weber, *The Protestant Ethic and the Spirit of Capitalism*, Penguin Classics (2002), c) R. H. Nelson, *Reaching for Heaven on Earth*, Rowman & Littlefield (1993), pp. 27-84.

[10] Landes, pp. 3-28.

[11] R. Wilson, *Economics, Ethics and Religion Jewish, Christian and Muslim Exonomic Thought* (New York University Press, 1997).

2.2 Judaic Law[12]

Judaism is the oldest religion in the Middle East, with over 3,000 years of tradition. Christianity built on the Jewish tradition and Islam respects the teachings of the prophets. The tradition of Judaism rests on two main sources. First, the Torah, the first five books of the Bible, is thought to be written by Moses. It is the "highest and best" evidence of the rules coming directly from God. The Ten Commandments and the teachings in Leviticus are prime examples. Second, the Talmud contains refinements and interpretations of the Law written by Judaic scholars, e.g. Scribes and Pharisees. The rationale for the Talmud is that "the Law is no longer in Heaven." In other words, it has been left to scholars to determine how the Law should apply to everyday interactions. Jewish law, the *Halakha,* is therefore fluid and is basically a matter of majority rule, with greater weight given to the better known rabbis. Oral tradition, the *Mishnah,* and 6,000 pages of commentary during the Babylonian captivity, were also critical to the development of Jewish tradition.

Devout Jews believed that wealth and prosperity are direct gifts from God as a blessing for living a moral life. Conversely, famine and poverty were considered divine punishments for a sinful life. Although Judaic law encouraged honest labor to accumulate wealth, accumulating excess wealth was discouraged. Here was also an obligation to contribute to the welfare of the community by charitable contributions to less fortunate individuals and families. This encouraged others to prosper, indicating that their economy was not a zero sum game. Every Jew was also directed to spend time studying the Torah to learn God's commands to live a virtuous life. Judaic Law does impose a number of specific restrictions on economic activity.

---

[12] Ibid., pp. 22-66.

2.2.1 Labor and Production[13]

In modern economic theory, labor is classified as a factor of production, along with capital and resources. Judaic scholars recognized the uniqueness of labor, since it involves the lives of human beings. Jews are encouraged to work for the economic necessities of life. However, they are forbidden to work on the Sabbath and the eight festival days during the year. Even slaves had to be treated fairly. If a slave lost an eye or a tooth due to a blow from his master, the Code of the Covenant declared that he had to be set free.

Land is another factor of production for the Agriculture Industry. The concept of Sabbatical originated from the command to leave the land fallow every seventh year. Trust in God is an essential element, i.e. that He will provide an abundant harvest in the sixth year, sufficient to last until the eighth year's harvest. Laborers would find other occupations and study the Torah. (Sabbatical leave still survives in Academia.) There is also an aspect of charity in this law. Indigent people had access to the land in the sabbatical year in order to forage for food. Every 50th year was a Jubilee, where land was returned to its original owners. Underlying this teaching is the belief that land was a gift from God and should not be sold permanently. Acquisition of land was in effect a long-term lease, with a return to the owner or the owner's family in the Jubilee year.

Talmudists treated contracts between employer and laborer as any other contract. Both parties had to fulfill their obligations or be found in default and subjected to paying damages. Labor unions

---

[13] a) M. Tamari, *With all Your Possessions: Jewish Ethics and Economic Life*, Jason Aronson (1998), pp, 127-58,

b) Ohrenstein, R. A., *Economic Analysis in Talmudic Literature: Rabbinic Thought in the Light of Modern Economics*, E. J. Brill (1992) pp. 114-31.

and guilds were permitted, but could not use their monopoly power to seriously damage the community or deprive non-members of their livelihood.

2.2.2 Envy and Theft [14]

Three of the Ten Commandments forbid coveting and stealing. Judaic Law did not consider theft as a major offense and it was not punished by maiming or imprisonment. Restitution was the remedy for this crime, sometimes requiring a four- or five-fold repayment. (Mr. Madoff might have some difficulty with this.) However, covetousness and theft were considered "gateway crimes," which could lead to violent crimes like robbery and murder.

Merchants were commanded to use honest weights and measures (Lev. 19:36). The Torah is quite specific about the exact weights and measures to emphasize the seriousness of the crime. A problem with this type of theft is that quantification at the consumer level is difficult. Many anonymous consumers can be cheated out of different amounts. Face-to-face restitution is almost impossible. Rabbinic courts adopt fines as the remedy for this type of fraud. Modern day weights and measures are enforced by a combination of consumer complaints and statistical sampling. Misrepresentation of products or services constitutes another form of theft. Numerous practices to make defective, or even hazardous, products attractive were forbidden in the rabbinic and secular courts. The prohibitions were extended to unwise or deceptive business advice. Halakha laws also provided special protection to the disadvantaged, who did not have the economic or political power to defend their interest. Widows, orphans, and strangers are examples of individuals qualifying for this special

---

[14] Tamari, pp. 31-52.

treatment. Even private property rights were limited to provide a social safety net for the disadvantaged. The community could tax the wealthy to provide subsistence to the poor. Failure to provide sustenance and opportunity for the disadvantaged was thought to be the sin of Sodom and Gomorrah by the Jewish sages.

2.2.3 Interest and Usury [15]

The Torah forbids charging interest on a loan to a fellow Jew (Exod. 22:24) and referred to the practice as extortion. An interest-free loan was considered a mitzvah (righteous act) by Halakhic authorities. Such generous acts provided opportunities for those less well off, resulting in a more prosperous community. There is some dispute about whether this prohibition applied only to fellow Jews or to all loans. In modern times, it is difficult to imagine why anyone would assume the risk of such a transaction without a corresponding reward. However, in tightly bound Jewish communities, the risk was greatly reduced. Failure to repay a debt was a major sin in the eyes of rabbinic courts. One tradition compared it to the sin of idolatry. The debtor could lose all his possessions by a ruling of these courts. These injunctions reduced the risk in the tightly knit Jewish communities to a low level.

Modern societies are much more heterogeneous. Jewish merchants and rabbis saw the necessity of charging interest of non-Jews who were not subject to the rulings of rabbinic courts. In medieval Europe, Jewish bankers became primary moneylenders. This was enabled by the stricter ban on interest taught by the Catholic Church. Financial houses, such as Rothschild, Oppenheimer, and Goldsmith grew to dominate the industry. Modern interest theory considers interest level to be a

---

[15] a) Tamari, pp. 139-206, b) Ohrenstein, pp. 132-6.

function of risk. Individuals with a history of dishonesty, or making poor choices, are assigned a lower credit score. Fortunately, these individuals may work to improve their scores by practicing responsible behavior over a specified period of time. A number of laws forbidding usury, or "excessive interest," have been passed throughout history. However, making the laws too stringent has occasionally resulted in high risk individuals losing all access to loans.

2.2.4 A Fair Price [16]

Sages in the Jewish triune have recognized that prices are a function of supply and demand, and that the market price is generally a fair price. They did acknowledge that supply shortages could disrupt normal markets in two ways: 1) Batzoret, where supply was maintained, but distribution was disrupted. The solution was to allow the market forces to restore equilibrium in the short run. 2) Kafna, where supply was destroyed by some catastrophe. In this case, intervention was necessary to relieve suffering.

A distinction was made between essentials, such as food or wine, and non-essentials, such as jewelry. Prices for essentials were monitored more closely and could only be sold locally by growers and manufacturers. Traders and distributors were only entitled to a profit if they added tangible value to a product. Charging more than 1/6 (16.5%) was considered excessive profit. How many companies today would be happy with a 16.5% return on sales? Table 2.1 displays recent returns for some public companies. Luxury goods, such as diamonds and silk, were not as heavily regulated. Merchants were free to charge whatever the market would bear.

---

[16] Ohrenstein, pp. 35-56.

Table 2.1 Profit Margins of Some Selected Companies[*]

Values are in billions of US $

Company	Sales	Gross Income	% Mark-up	Net Income	% Return on Sales
General Mills	17.6	6.11	35%	1.22	7 %
Wal-Mart	485	120.6	25 %	16.18	3 %
Coca-Cola	43.65	26.32	60 %	7.35	17 %
McDonald's	25.41	15.46	66 %	4.50	18 %
Gap Inc.	16.40	6.24	38 %	1.26	8 %
Pfizer	48.85	35.69	73 %	6.95	14 %
Tiffany	4.25	2.52	59 %	0.48	11 %
Coach Inc.	4.19	2.91	69 %	0.40	10 %

[*]Data selected from http://www.marketwatch.com for year 2015

2.2.5 Competition[17]

Judaic Law recognized that competition was beneficial to the community, since it kept prices low for consumers. Price fixing, cartels, and monopolies were frowned upon and often considered to be theft. Modern anti-trust laws are based on the same concepts. There were, however, some circumstances in which rabbinic authorities would intervene to protect sellers. For example, a bumper crop would reduce prices and leave sellers with unsold crops. The normal reaction of farmers would be to plant less the following year, which could result in a shortage.

---

[17] a) Tamari, pp. 61-125, b) Ohrenstein, pp. 57-68.

Rabbis would often buy surplus crops to encourage more planting. Current government policies use this rationale to impose price supports.

In some special cases, competition was discouraged, or even banned. Halakhic Law differentiated between reduced profits and destruction of one's livelihood. For example, an existing business in a community is likely to lose business if a competing business were to relocate from another city or country. Halakhic law would say the new business should be welcomed. (Remember the sin of Sodom.) The community would benefit since the two businesses would compete to offer better prices, quality, and service. However, if it is determined that the new entrant had some advantage that would put the established firm out of business, the new entrant would be blocked. This ban would be only for a defined time period to allow the existing firm to adjust.

Talmudic scholars recognize that innovation is often a double-edged sword. Productivity gains from new technology benefit the community in the form of increased supply and lower prices. However, workers using the obsolete technology could lose their jobs, an event that economists refer to as "transition cost." Rabbis might ban the innovation until the displaced workers can find other employment.

Even though monopolies are sometimes detrimental to the community, Judaic tradition respects the rights to intellectual property. The theory is that artists, authors, and inventors are allowed to enjoy the rewards of their labors. These talented individuals might not be motivated if their work could be simply imitated by free riders. Rabbinic courts regarded this imitation as theft, and protected the creators for a period of time. Modern patent, copyright and trademark laws follow the same reasoning.

Not surprisingly, Jews have been at the forefront of industries such as publishing, entertainment, and journalism.

2.2.6 The Worth of a Human Life [18]

In ancient times, slavery was widely practiced. Following wars, victorious countries would carry off male and female inhabitants to use as slaves. The Jews had experienced both sides of this situation, which may have influenced more humane Halakhic laws for the treatment of slaves. However, since slaves were an economic factor of production, sages sought to establish a value for their loss. The Jewish tradition of restitution for crimes or negligence made this important. Initially, a value of 30 shekels was established for all slaves, regardless of age or sex. This value was gradually refined to correspond to economic reality. Male slaves between 20 and 60 years of age were valued at 30 shekels. Women of childbearing age were worth 30 shekels. After age, 60 women were more valuable than men, because they could teach domestic skills to younger women.

Over time, the concept of economic value for human life was expanded to indentured servants and then, to free people. The concept was also widened to include injuries that would reduce the productive capacity of an individual. Damages, under current liability laws, are partially calculated based on lost income and other productive life functions.

The Talmud took a further revolutionary step by introducing the concept of the "valueless value." This idea states that even an individual with no productive economic value, has a monetary value, i.e. a moral value because he/she is a living human being. Welfare economics is a discipline based on this tradition. Essentially, this is a bridge between social and economic justice.

Judaic tradition in totality does not appear to favor one economic system; it balances work ethic and individual desires to gain

---

[18] Ohrenstein, pp. 113-130.

wealth against the welfare of the community. The vision is that acquiring wealth is good, as long as it also helps everyone to prosper. The Calvinist faith, which we shall examine in the next section, appears to be very close to these beliefs.

2.3 Christianity[19]

A reading of the four Gospels could give the impression that Jesus was indifferent, or even hostile, to the accumulation of wealth as read in the parable of Lazarus and the rich man (Luke 16: 19-31) and the episode of the wealthy young man who failed to give away everything to follow Jesus (Mark 10: 17-31). To drive home the point, Jesus said, "It is easier for a camel to go through the eye of a needle than for a rich man to enter the kingdom of God." Economists may recognize the latter story as an example of opportunity cost. The young man passed up the opportunity to follow Jesus and witness the greatest teachings and miracles in human history.

Given the above examples, one might conclude that Jesus was opposed to wealth-seeking behavior. However, in other teachings, He used examples, such as the parable of the talents (Matt. 25: 14-30) or the men who sold everything they had to buy a pearl or treasure (Matt: 13: 44-46). Today, we would call these men speculators, but Jesus portrays them as rational acts. Of course, this is an analogy to seeking the Kingdom of Heaven. An alternative thesis is that Jesus regarded wealth as a gift from God, adequately dealt with under Judaic Law. He had pledged not to change anything in the Law (Matt: 5: 17-19). Judaic Law would have vilified the rich man, who lived an ostentatious life, while a beggar starved at his gate. (Remember again the sin of Sodom.) Jesus' disciples were called to an even higher spiritual standard,

---

[19] Wilson, pp. 68-114.

e.g. love your enemies. A fair summary of His teachings can be found in Chapter 6 of Luke's Gospel.

The early Christian Church adopted a communal lifestyle, where they shared all things in common (Acts 4: 34-37). This is often cited as a model for a Marxist economy (from each according to his ability, to each according to his need). However, the major difference is that sharing in the early Christian Church was voluntary for all members. Of course some could nit-pick and cite the case of Ananias and Sapphira (Acts 5: 1-10). It's somewhat ironic that Marx would condemn faith as "the opiate of the people," and that communist governments would suppress religious freedom. The disciples also believed that Jesus would return during their lifetime. Then, who would need worldly possessions? But even among these highly-motivated early followers, resolve began to wear thin. Paul had to admonish slackers that whoever didn't work, didn't eat (2 Thess. 3: 10).

For a millennium, the Christian Church spread throughout the Middle East, Europe, and into Asia. The tradition thrived in spite of persecution, torture, and martyrdom. There were occasional disputes among the far-flung dioceses and patriarchies. In 1054, there was a serious split between the Eastern Churches and the Roman See. Some Greek Communities remained loyal to Rome[20]. Later splits occurred with the Church of England and the Protestant Reformation. Slightly different attitudes toward business ethics developed after these separations.

2.3.1 The Scholastic Tradition[21]

---

[20] For a brief history of this schism, see http://en.wikipedia.org/wiki/Melkite_Catholic_Church#Name_of_the_Church.
[21] O. Langhohn, *The Legacy of Scholasticism in Economic Thought* (Cambridge University Press, 1998).

For the first 1,500 years, Christian tradition was composed by weaving the threads of the New Testament and the articulated rationality of the Scholastics into Canon Law. This process was rather lumpy. There was a great deal of debate among the Church intelligentsia. The central themes for these discussions were natural law, free will, and the teachings of Jesus. A great deal of the rationality was based on the ethics of Aristotle[22], and the various compilations of Roman law[23]. Part of the confusion in debates may have been caused by variations in translating critical terminology from Greek to Latin. Augustine [24] and Thomas Aquinas [25] were the most notable figures in Scholasticism.

Aristotle discussed the concept of will and the fact that compulsion could mitigate freedom of an individual's will. Compulsive force could be 1) Violence or the threat of violence, or 2) Force of nature. An example of the latter is a ship's captain who throws cargo overboard in a storm. It is an act he would not will normally, but he does it to save his ship. The Scholastics extended compulsion into economic circumstances. An individual, who is starving, might be compelled by a merchant to pay an extravagant price for food. Scholastics determined that a "fair price" was determined by bargaining between a non-coerced buyer and a non-coerced seller. Any price significantly different was considered a sin of theft by the benefited individual. As the Tradition developed a distinction developed between necessities and luxuries. The "fair price" for luxuries was whatever a seller and buyer could get, in the absence of extortion.

---

[22] Aristotle, *Aristotle Niomachean Ethics* (Focus Publishing, 2008).
[23] P. du Plessis, *Textbook on Roman Law*, Third ed. (Oxford University Press, 2005).
[24] Langholm, pp. 43-57.
[25] Ibid., pp. 57-137.

Saint Ambrose extended the argument of compulsion to extend to charging interest (usury), describing it as robbery[26]. He based his reasoning on the book of Ezekiel which suggested that usury was equivalent to violent crime and abuse of the poor (Ezek. Ch.18). The Scholastics also invoked Jesus, who taught that a man should lend not expecting any return (Luke 6:35). It was assumed that the borrower paid interest against his will. A great irony was that Ambrose became the patron saint of Milan, the financial center of Italy. The prohibition by the Church allowed the Jews to build a great financial industry in Europe.

Scholastic views on labor developed later than the preceding areas of just price and interest. In the Middle Ages, slavery and servitude were widely accepted means for obtaining labor. A theory of a just wage was developed along the same line as the just price. The commonly accepted wage was considered to be whatever other masters were paying. It was assumed that an underpaid servant could find another position that would pay the going rate. This condition was true in a competitive market, free of coercion and collusion. There were also conditions in which a skilled worker could coerce an individual for whom he/she worked. For example, a skilled physician could charge an excessive fee to save a dying patient. The Scholastics would consider this an injustice.

Worland has postulated linkages between Scholasticism and the discipline of Welfare Economics,[27] based on Aquinas' teachings on the just price. Natural law concepts can also be applied to economics. The Law of Supply and Demand is as predictive as the Law of Gravity (see Appendix B). Sellers seek the highest price while buyers seek the lowest. In a perfect market, a just price is

---

[26] Ibid., pp. 59.

[27] S. T. Worland, *Scholasticism and Welfare Economics* (University of Notre Dame Press, 1967).

established. Disturbing this price by regulation, monopoly, or collusion will reduce the efficiency of the market. Setting the price too low will cause some sellers to withhold their product. A price that is too high will cause some buyers to walk away. Thomas Aquinas taught that natural law drives man to seek perfect happiness, primarily to live in harmony with God's will. On the physical side, he acknowledges that man should seek to acquire his needs and wants, as befit his station in life. Welfare economics concerns itself with 1) Maximizing the value of society's output, for example the GDP, 2) The just distribution of income, and 3) Maximizing the marginal utility of products. We will explore welfare economics in subsequent chapters.

2.3.2. The Protestant Economic Tradition

The Protestant Revolution was a rebellion against the repressive control and legalism that had developed in the Catholic Church. Some of this was aggravated by the entanglement of the Church with some European governments. Rigid doctrines were replaced by individual interpretation of scripture. Not surprisingly, this led to a multiplicity of Protestant Christian denominations. Unfortunately, when governments established an "official church," minority sects were often persecuted. Some of these sects settled in North America. The Founding Fathers of the United States considered this when they wrote the First Amendment.

Given the above situation, it is difficult to define a single "Protestant Ethic." The Anglican Church, apart from divorce, remained quite close to the teachings of the Catholic Church. This may have been due to the reluctance of Henry VIII to anger the king of France. Martin Luther rejected the Catholic belief that good works can assist in man's salvation[28]. However, he retained faith in God's grace and mercy. He also strongly condemned charging interest for the use of money. In these latter beliefs, he was closely aligned with Saint Paul. Luther's concept of "the calling" was that the faithful should accept God's will and perform their worldly duty to the best of their ability. This could explain the strong work ethic in Germany, Switzerland, and the Netherlands.

The "spirit of capitalism" pre-dated the Protestant Reformation, and was practiced by merchants, craftsmen, and bankers. Many of them spent their gains on luxuries and personal indulgences. This wealth-seeking behavior was condemned by most major religions. Weber has described the evolution of worldly Protestant asceticism as something completely different[29]. John Calvin was the most influential figure, but was also aligned with the Puritans and some Baptist sects. Wealth-seeking behavior was given a stamp of approval, as long as it was aligned with the will of God. The believer, however, practiced a frugal lifestyle, worked hard, and was scrupulously honest. In the Protestant ethic, hard work served two purposes. It allowed the capitalist to earn enough to support his family, and kept him too busy to experience temptation. The downside was that the accumulated wealth itself exposed him to temptation. Wesley recognized this, and suggested giving generously to those who are less fortunate.

Thomas Hobbes, one of the great thinkers of the late Scholastic period of the seventeenth century, recognized the importance of self-interest in economics[30]. He considered this an evil impulse that had to be restrained by a strong government authority. John Locke, the product of a Puritan family, believed that self-interest

---

[28] M. Weber, pp. 39-51.
[29] Ibid., pp. 54-125.
[30] http://en.wikipedia.org/wiki/Thomas_Hobbes

Gerard L. Hasenhuettl

was a positive influence[31]. He maintained the belief of Calvin that a self-disciplined individual could attain this instinct without the direction of government. Locke also kept the work ethic of Luther and wove in reason and natural law of Aquinas. A third strand was added, incorporating the scientific approach of Newton[32]. Subsequent thinkers, such as St. Simon, proposed a secular "Church of Newton," where math and science would replace revelation and tradition.

2.3.3. Liberation Theology[33]

Most Americans were unfamiliar with Liberation Theology before the Presidential Election of 2008. During the campaign, Rev. Jeremiah Wright, Barack Obama's pastor, received attention in the press for several controversial remarks. As in most political campaigns, both sides raced to define Liberation Theology, but did so in a superficial manner. This led to the belief that this was a radical anti-American Marxist religious sect. In reality, Liberation Theology (LT) is much more complex.

Origins of LT are difficult to define, but it first gained publicity with Catholic missionaries, working among the poor in South and Central America during the 1960's. Some of them became associated with revolutionaries, and several were killed by government forces or militia "death squads." Oscar Romero, the Bishop of El Salvador, was one of the most prominent martyrs.

The missionaries in South America focused on Jesus' teaching to serve the poor. Perhaps the teaching is best summarized by the words, "inasmuch as ye have done it unto one of the least of these

---

[31] http://en.wikipedia.org/wiki/John_locke
[32] Nelson, *Reaching for Heaven on Earth*, loc. cit., pp. 114-121
[33] Rowland (ed.), A. C., *The Cambridge Companion to Liberation Theology*, Cambridge University Press, 1999.

my brethren, ye have done it unto me" (Matt 25: 35-40). Liberation theology established the "privilege (priority) of the poor" as a core principle. However, the movement broadened out to embrace the oppressed, such as blacks, women, lower castes, and indigenous people. It's easy to understand why the poor and oppressed can identify with a suffering, crucified Messiah; however, the movement also defined the concept of "spiritual poverty." It applies to those who are preoccupied with acquiring wealth and neglect their moral obligation to serve the poor. Many missionaries have taken a vow of poverty to avoid falling into this trap.

One of the most effective tactics used by liberationists in South America was the establishment of basic ecclesial communities. The principle of "Hear, Judge, Act" was employed. Communities would gather and listen to the problems of their neighbors. They would discuss the problem and define a plan to solve it. For example, water and sanitation facilities in a neighborhood might be grossly inadequate. The community would decide what needed to be done. Action might involve pressuring political leaders to accept and act on their recommendations.

Liberation theology became controversial and divisive, when some of its activists began to adopt some Marxist principles. Class analysis was a tool that they felt was particularly useful. Of course they aligned themselves with the proletariat, rather than the oppressive bourgeois class. Pope St. John Paul II, who had experienced the repressive tyranny of a communist system, sternly rebuked his clergy. Ironically, liberation theologians faced severe problems when they won. For example, when the Kampuchea Vanguard workers party overthrew the Cambodian government, it opened the door for the murderous Pol Pot regime[34]. The Sandinistas failed to produce a workable economic plan after they

---

[34] Ibid., pp. 40-41.

came to power in Nicaragua. History is still being written in Venezuela, where Hugo Chavez was elected President. Unfortunately, the people there may have seen their last free election.

2.4 Islam[35]

Islam is the youngest, and possibly the fastest growing, of the world's major religions. The faith is based on the Koran, written by the prophet Mohammed. *Sharia* is the legal code developed from the Koran, similar to the development of the Talmud from the principles of the Torah. Economic life is an integral part of Islam. Over 1,400 of the 6,226 verses in the Koran deal with economic topics. After all, the Prophet was a trader in his early years. The first economic teachings were written in the eighth and ninth centuries. In the Middle Ages, Ibn Khaldun wrote extensively about ethics, economics and politics. Some have said that he is to Islam what Thomas Aquinas was to Catholicism. All of this being said, Islamic economic thought is not a monolith in the current era.

Modern Islamists approached the discipline from two different perspectives. Jurists and clerics started with Islamic principles and used them to define an economic system. Bani Sadr, briefly the president of Iran and the Muslim Brotherhood in Egypt, took this approach. Another school of thought started with western economic principles and adapted those to make them more acceptable to devout Muslims. Umer Chapra and Saved Naqvi, both Pakistani economists, are examples. Naqvi described Islamic ethics by observing the economic behavior of practicing Muslims. The four pillars he describes are *Tawhid* (unity), *Al Adi wal ihsan*

---

[35] Wilson, op. cit., pp. 115-63.

(equilibrium*), Ikbiy'ar* (free will), and *Fardh* (responsibility)[36]. Although specifics may vary depending on the country, we will examine some widely-held beliefs.

2.4.1 Private Property

Muslims believe that material possessions are a blessing and gift from Allah. Islam teaches that some individuals are blessed more than others are, and that believers should not covet another's possessions. However, an individual should not obsess over wealth accumulation. Devout Muslims are required to pray five times a day, so the tenets of their faith are never far from their consciousness. Faithful Islamists have a duty to share with others who are less fortunate. However, no government or other individual can demand this. It is a matter between the believer and Allah. They have been taught that Hell has been prepared for those who fail their duties to the poor. Muslims must also acquire their wealth honestly. Competition is permitted, but not if it is destructive to others. Monopolies and price fixing are forbidden. Hoarding is also considered evil because it reduces supply, causing higher prices, and hurting the community.

Further evidence of the acceptability of private property is the detailed system of inheritance from the Koran[37]. For example, a son inherits two parts of an estate to one for a daughter. Muslims are restricted from owning some types of businesses. For example, a business owner could manufacture jewelry, but not alcohol or pork products. Some governments have imposed taxes on wealth (as valorem), in order to build infrastructure and help the poor.

---

[36] Ibid., pp. 134-5.
[37] Ibid., pp. 117-8.

Gerard L. Hasenhuettl

2.4.2 Labor, Wages, and Trade

Like the Protestants, Muslims have a strong work ethic embedded in their faith. Bani Sadr defines three types of work: manual labor[38], administration, and innovation. Devout Muslims should do all three to have a balanced life and come closer to God. Balance is also a concept in Eastern philosophies, to be discussed later in this chapter. Employers are mandated to pay a fair wage, at least a subsistence amount. There is, however, no maximum amount that a person is allowed to make through honest and diligent work.

Adam Smith and Thomas Aquinas distinguished between productive labor. They did not consider trading as a value-added function and was therefore non-productive. The Koran contends that trade does add value. An Islamic trader offers knowledge and technical support as well as quality assurance. Non-productive activities are those which involve gambling or collecting *riba* (interest), which is viewed as deferred consumption. Merchants are commanded to use just weights and measures. Competition is allowed, but nothing should be done to harm one's competitors, such as hostile takeovers or monopolistic practices. Sharia courts would also prevent the strong from exploiting the weak. For example, a large supplier should not use his power to take advantage of a small customer. Beekun has outlined strategic planning methods for Islamic businesses to excel, while strictly adhering to Sharia Law[39]. He points out that corporate culture may be tightly linked to, and derived from, Islamic principles. For example, Savola, a Saudi food company, has four core principles. They are Amanah (honesty), Takwa (conscientiousness), Birr

[38] Sadr, A. B., *Work and the Worker in Islam*, Hamdami Foundation, Tehran, 1980.
[39] R.Beekun, I., *Strategic Planning and Implementation for Islamic Organizations*, International Institute of Islamic Thought, Hampton, VA, 2006.

(caring), and Mujahada (personal control). These core values, combined with modern techniques such as SWOT analysis, allowed this company to grow from a small oil processor to a billion-dollar company.

2.4.3 Islamic Finance Banking, and Investment[40]

Over the last forty years, there has been great interest in the area of Islamic finance. As the global economy and immigration of Muslims into non-Muslim countries have led to a demand for Islamic financial instruments, Islamic jurists tend to favor traditional Islamic practices. Economists trained in the west, prefer to start with currently used documents and modify them to render them Sharia-compliant. Results of these two approaches are not dramatically different. Two prohibitions in Sharia Law have profound effects on Islamic financial transactions. *Riba* (interest) is also prohibited in Judaic and Christian tradition. Gharar (risk or gambling) represents a profit (or loss) from unproductive work.

Mortgages and credit cards charge interest at a fixed rate and would be prohibited by Sharia Law. Islamic alternatives are necessary to allow Muslims to participate in the modern economy. A mortgage, for example, can be replaced by a *murabaha*, or multiparty salwa contract. In this case, the mortgagee (e.g., a bank) would buy the property from the seller, and then rent the property to the buyer. Essentially, this becomes a lease-purchase agreement. If the bank does not wish to own the property, it can buy through a Specialty Purpose Vehicle (SPV). An Islamic bond, or *sukk*ah, is commonly used for commercial finance. Thus holders are involved in a multi-party lease purchase agreement.

---

[40] M. El-Gamel, *Islamic Finance: Law, Economics, and Practice*, Cambridge University Press, 2006.

Islamic investors must screen their portfolio on a number of levels. They must exclude participation in companies that are involved with poor processing, alcohol production, or gambling. Since Gharar is forbidden, they must screen out stocks with large price fluctuations (high beta). As described above, they are prohibited from owning interest-bearing bonds. However, they may lend money to an entrepreneur in exchange for a share of the business' profits. In this case, the investor fulfills the role of a venture capitalist.

Traditional, western-style futures contracts are forbidden under Islamic law because they involve Gharar or excessive risk. In effect, parties are buying and selling commodities that they don't own, or don't yet exist. However, Sharia courts have carved out exceptions for groups that are adversely affected by not having access to these markets. For example, farmers often need to sell future crops in order to buy seeds. In these cases, jurists use a balancing test between benefits and detriments. Other *Salam* (forward) contracts, such as those involving paired commodities, are more controversial.

These Islamic instruments are more expensive than their standard counterparts for two reasons. Involvement of additional parties leads to increased transaction costs. Sharia jurists and lawyers must be involved to ensure that these innovative alternatives comply with both religious and secular laws. As these instruments become standardized, these costs may decrease. These multi-party vehicles also attract the scrutiny of government law enforcement agencies, since the special purpose vehicles look like shell companies, used by criminals to launder currency.

2.4.4 Insurance[41]

The use of insurance by Muslims could be viewed as a lack of trust in Allah. On the other hand, it can be justified as a prudent measure to reduce risk. Life insurance is forbidden. Islamic tradition teaches that the Umma (community of believers) should support surviving spouses and children.

Commercial property/casualty companies are often condemned by Sharia courts. Since these companies can statistically model risk, they can set their premiums to ensure maximum profitability. Thus they are profiting from the misfortune of others. Mutually-owned companies avoid this problem[42]. These companies are owned by the policy holders, who are able to decide how finances should be managed.

2.5 Eastern Religions

The Middle East religions we have examined so far are very similar in how they view God. He is anthropomorphic. They assign to God the same emotions possessed by humans. This is consistent with belief that we are created in God's image. Eastern religions describe God as a pure spirit and source of energy, or karma. Faiths of the Orient are concerned with harmony and balance. Reincarnation is widely accepted. The various religions have cross-pollinated in some countries. For example, Shintoism in Japan has been influenced by Buddhism and Confucianism. There does not appear to be a preference for a single system of political economy. Eastern religions have been used to rationalize both Marxism and capitalism. In this section we will seek to identify core beliefs concerning business ethics.

---

[41] Ibid., pp. 61-2, 147-62, 170-1.
[42] Ibid., pp. 173-4.

2.5.1 Hinduism

The Hindu tradition has been said to be the oldest living religion. The first *Vedic's*, or written teachings, date from 1700 to 1100 B.C. and oral tradition goes back even further. There is no single identifiable founder and many denominations have grown up over centuries. For this reason, there is a great deal of tolerance within Hinduism for diverse beliefs. There is even a faction of atheist Hindus. Most factions believe in *samsara,* a repeating cycle of birth, death, and rebirth. Believers strive for perfection in order to escape this cycle. Hinduism is the third most popular religion worldwide, behind Christianity and Islam. Teachings deal with behavior in many aspects of everyday life. We will focus on Arthashastra[43], or virtuous pursuit of wealth.

The Arthashastra dates back to the fourth century B.C. It was written as a pragmatic guide for rulers to enrich their people, wage war, and maintain control of their empires. Max Weber suggested that it is more ruthless than Machiavelli. Not surprisingly, the Arthashastra collides with the Dharmashastra, the book that defines everyday behavior for all Hindus. Part of this work deals with political economy, a guide to the monarch; on how to maximize prosperity for himself and his people. He is directed to lead by example. If a king is energetic and just, the people will behave in the same way. On the other hand, if he is lazy and corrupt, the people will follow his example, and the wealth of the nation will decline.

Jara (tax) was levied on production at a rate of one-sixth (O16.5%). This was a flat tax for all levels of income. In return, the taxpayers received protection and the right to vote. Kara for

---

[43] a) Kautalya, *The Arthashastra*, Penguin Books India, 1992. b) www.wikipedia.com/Arthashastra.

traders was one-tenth (10%), but the merchants also had to pay user fees, such as admission to markets. Imported goods were taxed to protect domestic producers.

Under the Arthashastra, the economic system was centrally planned and under the direction of the *Rajarshi* (king). However, the king's power was not absolute. A small council of ministers and advisors formed an oligopoly and decisions were made by consensus. The king was either elected by the people or selected by the oligopoly. Accession by the king's heirs was not automatic. Labor was divided into specialized groups and the early Hindu economy consisted of agriculture, mining, and forestry. Land and forests could be privately owned, but mines were owned by the government.

Specialization of labor was formalized in Indian tradition. The Hindu state assigned duties according to the *Varna* (socioeconomic groups) system. Four Varna's (castes) were defined: 1) *Brahmins* were the intelligentsia and served as teachers and priests; 2) *Kshatriyas* were kings, governors, and military personnel; 3) *Vaishyas* were cattle herders, agriculturists, and merchants; 4) *Shudras* were laborers, artisans, and service providers. The first two classes were provided with wide-ranging educational opportunities. Vaishya's received vocational training. Shudras had no access to formal education but could receive informal education at home. The responsibilities of the Kshatriyas were to manage efficient growth and to protect the weak from the strong. Individuals were encouraged to marry within their own Varna. This led to a stratified society; it was difficult to cross from one Varna to another.

2.5.2 Buddhism[44]

Like many ancient historical icons, the life of the Buddha has been the subject of disagreement among scholars. The consensus is that Siddhartha Gautama was born as a crown prince in northeast India and lived during the period 563-400 B. C. As a young man, he rejected the life of the palace to try to alleviate the suffering of the people. He tried living as an extreme ascetic, but found that suffering was unaffected. After more meditation, he began to travel and to teach the "middle path' (between self-indulgence and self-denial).

Buddhism retains core concepts of Hinduism, such as samsara and karma, but builds on these beliefs. The Four Noble Truths deal with the problem of *dukkha* (suffering): 1) Suffering is inevitable; 2) It is caused by ignorance of the nature of things; 3) An end to suffering is possible; 4) Dukkha can be ended by following the Noble Eightfold path of right view, understanding, intention, thought, speech, action, livelihood, effort, mindfulness, and concentration. These eight factors are interconnected and interdependent. Most Buddhists believe that negative karma can be purged by right living, chanting, and meditation. One departure from Hinduism is that there is no caste system in Buddhism. It is the most peaceful of the major religions, doing no harm to any sentient beings. For this reason, most Buddhists are vegetarians.

The "middle way" suggests that workers and businesses can legitimately earn money, providing that they engage in non-harmful occupations. They should not obsess on wealth, since it is so impermanent. In his informative and entertaining book, *The Diamond Cutter,* Geshe Roach tells about building a multi-million dollar business by applying Buddhist principles[45]. Roach teaches

---

[44] http://www.wikipedia.com/Buddhism.
[45] L. Roach and C. McNally, *The Diamond Cutter*, Doubleday, 2000.

the Buddhist principles of reaching one's full potential, much like a perfectly-cut diamond. This status is achieved by creating imprints on the subconscious mind through right thoughts, words, and actions. He poses 46 common business problems, and suggests that their origins lie within specific imprints.[46] The author suggests strategies to correct the faulty imprints for each problem.

2.5.3 Confucianism[47]

There is some debate about whether Confucian tradition should be considered a religion, philosophy, or system of ethics. It is likely a complex mosaic of all three. Confucius lived from 551-479 B.C. and served as a sage, teacher, and government official. His original teachings emphasized morality, family, and loyalty to legitimate authority. He proposed the "Silver Rule," a negative formulation of the Golden Rule ("What you do not wish to be done to yourself, do not do to others"). The Five Canons were written by Confucius, and served as a template for much subsequent Chinese tradition.

Confucius believed in a centralized government, led by officials of the highest moral and ethical character. This was aspirational, since most of his life was spent in a feudal society, not always ruled by men of superior character. He believed that if a king set a good example, the people would automatically follow. Orders would be unnecessary. A regional official asked Confucius what was the most important thing he could do for his people. "Enrich them," the sage replied. When asked about the next most important thing, the simple answer was, "educate them."

---

[46] Ibid., pp. 81-130.
[47] http://www.wikipedia/Confucianism.

Gerard L. Hasenhuettl

Confucian economic thought was driven by both ethical and rational principles[48]. For example, he defined the three factors of production as capital, land, and the virtuous man, the latter being the most important. Although he considered government control to be important, he also noted that businesses would migrate to where they were best treated. Confucius respected the free market, but sought to control prices by depressing demand. He stated, "Producers should be many; consumers should be few. Production should be rapid; consumption should be slow." Environmentalists should find this belief attractive.

Confucius had a long-term vision that morally upright people would all progress to a stage where they would all be equally wealthy and educated. He called it the Great Similarity. In this Utopian society, there would be no need for government, laws, or relationships. Everyone would be equal. This resembles the Buddhist principles discussed in *The Diamond Cutter*. The path to self-development lies in learning and hard work. In Confucius' time, government jobs were filled through competitive exams. This might be considered as the forerunner of the modern civil service exams. It is a practical application of the Confucian principle that a government should be run by the most capable people.

Confucianism was not confined to China, but influenced the cultures of other Asian countries[49]. In Japan, the social morality was fashioned by a weave of three religions: Shintoism, (native), Buddhism, and Confucianism[50]. Confucian teachings were incorporated into the *Bushida*, the code of the Samurai, as early as

---

[48] a) Chen, Huan-Chang, *The Economic Principles of Confucius and his School*, Vol. 1,, Bristol, Thoemme Press (2002),
   b) Ibid., Vol. 2, University Press of the Pacific (2003).
[49] Tu, Wei-ming (ed.), *Confucian Tradition in East Asian Modernity*, Harvard University Press (1996.
[50] Ibid., pp. 72-174.

46

the thirteenth century. In the late nineteenth and the first half of the twentieth centuries, morality yielded to nationalism, but Confucian beliefs and practices persisted. Governments in Korea and Taiwan were also supportive of Confucian principles[51]. Education professionals are highly respected members of the Confucian elite. Businesses used the concept of the extended family to socialize new employees into the organization. Hong Kong and Singapore, the other two mini-dragons, had strong Confucian values, but were heavily influenced by western values as they experienced economic growth.

2.5.4 Taoism[52]

China might be described as a country navigating through a myriad of paradoxes. Articles about traditional Chinese medicine share the pages of journals with papers on the latest drug targeting techniques. The centrally planned economy is evolving into free market capitalism. Tradition is rich with dichotomy of Confucianism versus Taoism.

Taoism is thought to have originated from the teachings of Laozi in the fourth century B.C. His inspired beliefs are published in the *Tao Te Ching* followed by a Canon and a number of commentaries. *Tao*, meaning way or path, is also described as the driving force of the universe. Components of the force are *Yin* and *Yang*, often symbolized by the dragon and the lamb. These are opposing forces, but they may interact to determine unknown outcomes. Staying in harmony with this force is the goal of Taoists. The three jewels of Taoism are compassion, moderation, and humility.

---

[51] Ibid., pp. 175-227.
[52] http://www.wikipedia.com/Taoism.

Gerard L. Hasenhuettl

In order to stay harmonized with Tao, believers follow the central tenet of *wu wei* (wei = action, wu = absence). It is also stated *wei wu wei* (action by inaction). This allows the forces of Tao to form the destiny of the faithful. This is remarkably similar to the teaching of Jesus concerning trust in God (Luke 12: 22-34): "So I tell you not to worry about the food you need to stay alive, or about the clothes you need for your body." Zhao discusses this concept thoroughly and uses a number of illustrations[53]. He points out that through inaction, things can still be accomplished. He also notes that the expression "take it easy" is a rough equivalent to "wu wei." Taoism believes that the best government is that which governs least. With little regulation, businesses can operate with great efficiency. It's the polar opposite of Confucianism, which believes in a strong central government. Neoconfucianism has been incorporating useful principles of Buddhism and Taoism.

2.6 Humanism

Humanism is a term that refers to a number of heterogeneous groups that believe that man is a rational being that has the power to improve society. It is a belief that a moral code should be established by observation, empirical data, and reason. Scientists often say, "In God we trust. Everyone else must bring data."

Scholars have found traces of humanism as far back as 1700 B. C. in the Middle East, China, and India. The pre-Socratic Greeks, Thales and Xenophanes explained the world in terms of human reason, rather than myth and tradition. Their writings are reflected in the teachings of Plato and Aristotle. After the Dark Ages, Humanism bloomed during the Renaissance. Petrarch, whose role model was Cicero, was likely the first Humanist of the period. Two parallel directions emerged during the Renaissance: 1) The

---

[53] Q. Zhao, *Do Nothing & Do Everything*, Paragon House (2010).

ad fonts (back to the sources) approach led to detailed textual analysis of pre-Christian Greek and Roman writings; 2) A dedication to improving the quality of life and level of education of humanity. Through the 18th and 19th centuries, Humanism began to split reason away from religion. Humanism morphed into a "religion of mankind."

In 1929, Charles Francis Potter formed the Humanist Society of New York. Notable members were Julian Huxley and Albert Einstein. Potter went on to publish *Humanism: A New Religion*[54]. In 1933, a group met at the University of Chicago to proclaim *The Humanist Manifesto*[55]. Humanism was declared to be a new religion based on science and reason, rather than divine revelation and religious tradition. It called for the abolition of a profit-driven economy and replacement of competition by cooperation. This was softened in later versions of the Manifesto, possibly because of human rights abuses of communist governments. The Manifesto was modified in 1973, and again in 2003. New positions included endorsing abortion, gay rights and assisted suicide.

The Amsterdam Declaration was issued by the International Humanism and Ethical Union at its 50th Congress in 2002[56]. Seven principles were put forward (points are abstracted):

- Humanism is ethical and based on intrinsic human reason. It advocates the greatest possible freedom, consistent with rights of others.

---

[54] C. F. Potter, *Humanism: A New Religion*, Simon & Schuster (1930).
[55] http://www.americanhumanist.org/WhoWeAre/About_Humanism/Humanist Manifesto_I
[56] Herrick, loc. cit., pp. 101-2.

- Humanists believe in the free inquiry of science, tempered by human reason. Divine intervention is deemed unnecessary.

- Humanists are dedicated to democracy, human rights, and the greatest possible development of each individual.

- Humanism insists on individual freedom and individual responsibility. Education should be free from indoctrination.

- Humanism is an alternative to dogmatic religion.

- Humanism values the creativity and inspiring power of art, literature, and music.

- Humanism offers a lifestyle of rational and ethical values to everyone, everywhere.

Nelson described a "heaven on earth" society, where all needs would be met, and as a result, conflict would be unnecessary[57]. The economic system would be centrally planned, with decisions made using laws of economics. Nelson described the economists as high priests. This future society is cast in the mold of Humanism; it has previously been described by Confucius and Marx.

Although Humanism and organized religions have several beliefs in common, prospects for cooperation are hampered by their disagreement on theism. Debates often turn into *ad hominum* attacks. Humanists argue that atheism should be the default position. However, there is no default position in the scientific

---

[57] R. H. Nelson, *Economics as Religion: From Samuelson to Chicago and Beyond*, Penn State University Press (2001)..

method. One formulates a hypothesis, and then designs an experiment to test it. Since no one is yet able to see or measure God, the hypothesis is untestable. We are thus left with our individual beliefs.

2.7 Differences and Common Ground

The world's religions vary in their concept of God, or even the existence of God. Their beliefs about how the economy should be structured also diverge. Confucianism, Hinduism, Humanism, and some Catholics support a centrally-planned economy. Judaism, Taoism, Islam, and many Protestant denominations tend to favor free enterprise. However, there are some common teachings. For example:

- All human beings should be free.

- All people should be allowed to develop to their maximum potential.

- Those who are rich should help those who are less fortunate.

In Chapter 4, we will attempt to reconcile common moral and ethical beliefs with practical economic principles.

51

Chapter 3

Significant Events in Economic History

"Life must be lived in the forward direction,
but can only be understood in reverse."
-Soren Kierkegaard-

3.1 Introduction

Economic history is a tale of innovation; humans used their intellect to solve problems. At first, progress appears to have been slow. Humans spent millions of years in the Stone Age. Skipping forward, the steam engine took about 100 years to progress to the turbine era. Today's high-tech products can become obsolete in only a few years. This acceleration can be explained by the myriad of enabling technologies developed through history. We do stand on the shoulders of giants.

Innovation can be categorized as either continuous or discontinuous. Continuous innovation is a sequential improvement of a product, process, or service. Constant improvements are made in quality, cost reduction, and productivity (more, better, faster). Discontinuous innovation is a game changer. It makes an existing product, process, or service obsolete.

Since the beginning, our individual well-being has been linked to our economic situation. If we can understand where we've been, we might be able to plot a course for our future. The story of civilization is remarkably uneven in both time and geographic regions. Periods of prosperity have been followed by times wrought with trouble. Great empires rose and fell. An excellent and efficient source on this topic is the work of Cameron and Neal[58].

3.2 Ancient History

Ancient history has been divided according to the tools and weapons used in that period. The Stone Age (3,000,000 – 3,000 B. C.), the Bronze Age (2500 – 800 B. C.), and the Iron Age (700-180 B. C.) have been loosely defined. The dates are approximate and do not apply evenly across all geographic regions. For example, some parts of Africa seem to have transitioned from the Stone Age directly to the Iron Age. In other regions, stone tools co-existed with bronze and iron tools.

3.2.1 The Stone Age

Humans are thought to have inhabited the earth for about 3 million years. Historical written language has only been known for about 4,500 years. How can we then determine what economic

---

[58] R. Cameron and L. Neal, *A Concise Economic History of the World: From Paleolithic Times to the Present*, Fourth Edition, Oxford University Press (2003).

conditions were in the preceding periods? There are only indirect clues available.

Anthropologists and archaeologists have made heroic efforts to identify preserved objects, date them, and interpret their utility. Tools, weapons, and utensils tell a story about how early man lived. Of course, there are significant difficulties with this method. Fossils and objects are degraded or destroyed by nature, and as a result, the fossil record is incomplete. Scientists debate about methodology and conclusions. New discoveries can change previous interpretations. But it is the most objective evidence available.

Another interesting technique was described by Sahins[59]. Primitive aboriginal tribes, still living in the Stone Age, were studied to determine their economic habits. They were hunter gatherers, living on wild game, fruits, and vegetation. Contrary to expectations, they did not have to work hard to support themselves. This is a primitive example of supply and demand. Game and wild plants were abundant, relative to the population. Since hunting and gathering free goods was so easy, there was little incentive to innovate. There were also no enabling technologies. Use and control of fire may have been the first.

The Stone Age was divided into three periods, although there are two systems that have subtle differences. One will be described for simplicity. The Paleolithic Age saw the appearance of *Homo erectus* who chipped rocks to fashion cutting tools. The Mesolithic Age was the domain of Neanderthal man. Both periods show evidence of hunter-gatherer economics. In the Neolithic Age, there was a revolutionary development. Man began to cultivate crops and agriculture. Tools in this period were

---

[59] M. Sahins, *Stone Age Economics*, Second Edition, Routledge Taylor & Francis (2003).

constructed using stone, wood, and bone. Agriculture diversified the food supply and enabled establishment of larger settlements. Since there was no written history to this time, innovators, if they were known at all, were only known through spoken tradition. It is interesting to speculate how early humans first learned to preserve and control fire.

3.2.2 The Bronze Age

Somewhere around the third millennium B.C., some with no knowledge of chemistry or the Periodic Table, discovered that heating copper ore resulted in a metal that could be cast into shapes. Further experiments found that copper-tin alloys produced bronze, which was a harder metal. Control of fire and firing of ceramics were the preceding innovations that enabled the birth of metallurgy.

Many other developments occurred during the Bronze Age, such as written records, mathematics, and astronomy. Two noteworthy cultures were located in Babylon and the Indus Valley. Written languages were Sumerian and a precursor to Sanskrit, respectively. Agriculture was sufficiently improved to allow the creation of cities. Innovations were diffused throughout the Mediterranean countries by the Phoenicians and later by the Greeks. Of course, this resulted in improvements to boat building and navigation technologies.

3.2.3 The Iron Age

Replacement of bronze by iron is typical of innovation materials science. When a material is in short supply, is too expensive, or has undesirable properties, an innovator will find a substitute. Copper was useful for some applications but was too soft for others, for example, weapons. Alloying copper with tin produced a harder metal. Bronze had to be cast and worked or stamped cold. In the late Bronze Age, tin became a scarce commodity. Iron was a hard metal and could be worked hot and pounded into shape by a blacksmith.

Early in the period, iron pieces were rare, and owned by nobility. In Egypt an iron dagger and ax were found in the tomb of a Pharaoh. Iron was scarce because it was more difficult to smelt iron than it was for other metals. Special furnaces had to be developed and the art of smiting had to be learned. Later in the Age, iron was combined with carbon to produce steel, which had superior properties for a number of applications.

3.2.4 The Era of Empires and Dynasties

As time passed, societies grew more complex. Cities became city-states and then kingdoms. Through military conquest, powerful empires and dynasties appeared. These mega-governments possessed great resources and economies of scale, which allowed them to create massive structures. Pyramids in Egypt, aqueducts in Rome, the Great Wall of China, and the Acropolis in Greece are examples. Large military contingents maintained law and order. Significant architectural and engineering innovations were used to enable construction of structures that endured for thousands of years. One example is the discovery of the Pozzolanic reaction of calcium hydroxide (limestone) and silica (lava ash) to form cement. The Roman Pantheon was built with this material.

Economic demographics were quite lopsided. The wealthy class comprised only about 5-10% of the population. The remaining 90-95% comprised the servile class (servants and slaves). Since there was such an abundance of cheap or free labor, little attention was given to productivity innovations. As the wealthy class grew in absolute numbers, pressure for greater wealth was placed on the empires. The easiest way to grow wealth was to conquer more territory and exact tribute and taxes from the people. As a result, the empire became overextended and indefensible. Dynasties in China were formed to unite the country. Then were torn apart by regional conflicts or by ambitions of local leaders. The empire/dynasty model persisted in China, Japan, India, and Korea into modern times. The Ming Dynasty had little respect for western technologies and did not adopt them. Japan, under the Samurai, adopted these innovations and set out to improve them[60].

When the Roman Empire began to crumble, the army could no longer provide security for traders. Bandits on land and pirates on the seas prowled the trade routes. To cope with these dangerous conditions, the *commenda contract* was developed. An older trader, unable to cope with the rigors of travel, would consign merchandise to a young vigorous man. After delivery and payment, the pair would split the profits. This is an important milestone in partnerships, capitalism, and contract law. It may also be a warning to large empires, where wealth is concentrated in the top few percent of the population, particularly where there is no path for the servile class to gain wealth.

3.3 The Dark Ages – or Were They?

The collapse of the Roman Empire resulted in the Manorial System throughout Europe. Individual estates were led by Nobles and manned by serfs. The expression of this era was: "No land without a lord, and no lord without land." Where central governments existed, their authority often ended at the gates of the manor.

---

[60] Landes, loc. cit., pp. 335-391

Gerard L. Hasenhuettl

Cameron takes issue with the term "dark ages," because it suggests that no progress was made during this time. Granted, culture and the arts were not flourishing, at least not until the reign of Charlemagne in the ninth century. However, innovation was quietly being practiced on the manors.

Disruption of the trade routes meant that individual manors had to become largely self-sufficient. Inventions had to be practical and were in the areas of agriculture and weaponry. Crop rotation was improved from two to three stages. The iron plow was useful for breaking up heavy soils. Horses and oxen were used to power the plows, and the manure was used for fertilizer. Horses were faster and stronger, but were more expensive to breed and feed. The calculation whether to use horses or oxen was an early example of agricultural economics.

Marauding invaders forced neighboring manors to cooperate. Innovations were diffused locally as weapons and crops were improved. Flexible defense arrangements were practiced, with one or more lords being subservient to another.

3.4 The Middle Ages and the Renaissance

Historians have debated when the Middle Ages began and ended. There was also disagreement about the impact of the Renaissance and whether it should be considered a separate period. For the purpose of discussing innovation, we will consider the entire period from 1000 to 1700 A.D. It was a time of wars, famine, religious strife, and political intrigue. More importantly, discoveries made during this period laid the foundations for later economic growth and higher standards of living.

During the twelfth and thirteenth centuries, more significant inventions appeared than in the previous thousand years. Windmills, spectacles, water clocks, and spinning wheels are examples. New business practices, such as double entry bookkeeping and letters of credit, to reduce the risk of commercial transactions were developed and refined. Islamic armies invaded the countries of Eastern Europe, disrupting trade routes to the Orient. In the late fifteenth century, Vasco de Gama sailed around the tip of Africa and Columbus sailed across the Atlantic. Intensive mapping and navigation techniques were developed to facilitate exploration.

The first 400 years saw the beginnings of urbanization. Agricultural innovations produced enough food to supply large cities. As food supplies increased and migration from the east continued, Europe's population grew. In the fourteenth century an epidemic known as the Black Death reduced the population by about one-third. Land became cheap, but labor became scarce. Serfs were unwilling to work for subsistence wages. Trade Guilds were organized in the cities. They controlled the training of apprentices, product quality, and standardization.

The Renaissance began in Florence in the fifteenth century, and then spread to other Italian cities. There was a rebirth of Roman and Greek philosophy, architecture, science, and medicine. Migration of Byzantine scholars, after the fall of Constantinople, added further knowledge. Renaissance thought crossed into France and then diffused into the rest of Europe. The principles of biology, chemistry, physics, and astronomy would enable future innovation.

3.5 Industrialization (First Industrial Revolution)[61]

As with other periods, there is little agreement on the starting and ending dates for the industrialization era. It is somewhat easier to describe the attitudes that characterized the period. The observations and ideas of the Renaissance were replaced by experimentation and product improvement. Production shifted from small shops and cottages to factories with large work forces. International trade increased, encouraged by the writings of Adam Smith and David Ricardo. Cameron listed three characteristics of industrialization:

- Mechanical power replacement of animal and human effort.
- Energy obtained from new sources, e.g. fossil fuels.
- New materials, not found in nature.

Inventions and ideas from the Middle Ages were incrementally improved and had an enormous impact on industrialization. A few examples can illustrate this point:

Spectacles, enabled by the science of optics, could correct the farsightedness caused by aging. Skilled craftsmen were unable to focus on objects that were close, as they got older. This made them slower and less skillful when doing precision tasks. Using spectacles to correct this defect could double the productive life of a skilled artisan.

Clocks were invented in the Middle Ages to democratize time, that is, to allow the average citizen to know the time of day. The first clock was the sundial. Obviously, it did not work when the sun was not shining, and did not account for seasonal variation. The water clock solved these problems, but its accuracy depended on the precision of manufacturing, temperature, and purity of the

---

[61] a) Landes, loc. cit., pp. 186-255, b) Cameron, loc. cit., pp. 219-289.

water. The mechanical clock proved to be superior to its predecessors. The first models were large, but incremental size reductions produced the pocket watch. Widespread knowledge of time dramatically improved coordination of production, transportation, and education. Families awoke to the sound of the factory whistle, as well as to the church bells.

Incremental innovations for the steam engine took about a century to achieve its maximum efficiency. The first models were based on reciprocating pistons and operated near atmospheric pressure. They were fueled by wood or coal. They were used to pump water out of mines. Models were developed to operate at higher pressures, yielding higher efficiency. Unfortunately, inadequate precision of fit between the piston and the cylinder posed a serious risk of explosion. Methods used to bore cannon barrels were applied to achieve closer tolerances.

As urbanization progressed, trade guilds were formed in the urban areas. They promoted quality and standardization, but they also produced low supply and high prices. Merchants, who sought to reduce costs and lower prices to gain competitive advantage, resorted to a practice known as "putting out." They would supply raw wool and cotton to non-guild spinners and weavers who lived outside the city. These low-cost artisans would convert these raw materials into finished cloth. These were home-based businesses, which led to the term "cottage industry." Weaknesses in this system were that delivery could be unreliable and quality was often inconsistent.

The Industrial Revolution created the factory system. Large numbers of workers were gathered into large buildings and worked the same hours. An advantage of co-location was closer supervision, which led to more reliable production and quality. Mechanical power was applied to processes such as spinning and weaving. Higher capital investment was required to purchase the machinery, but labor costs could be reduced. Larger operations also resulted in economies of scale. Other industries, such as metal processing, also adopted the factory system.

Systems of international trade were also refined. Ricardo proposed that nations should specialize in industries where they possessed a natural comparative advantage. Nations with abundant minerals could export them and import other products, such as food and clothing. Countries rich in capital should specialize in capital-intensive industries, such as steel production. Where labor was plentiful, labor-intensive industries should prosper. Some exceptions to Ricardo's rules occurred in practice. The United States, for example, was a capital-rich country that excelled in agriculture.

Nations varied in their pursuits of free trade versus protectionism. Great Britain followed the advice of Smith and Ricardo to embrace free trade. Since Britain was a first-mover to industrialization, it was an easy choice. France and other follower countries imposed tariffs to protect their fledgling industries. However, even Britain flirted with protective legislation, such as the Corn Laws and the Navigation Act.

3.6 The Second Industrial Revolution[62]

There is little agreement about starting and ending dates for either the first or second Industrial Revolution. History can be messy. Perhaps we can find a clue based on the nature of innovation for these periods. Both had a sufficient population of visionaries and experimentalists. However, the first Industrial Revolution involved individual technologies, such as steam power, metallurgy, and textiles. The second period was characterized by

---

[62] a) Landes, loc. cit., pp. 442-511, b) Cameron, loc. cit., pp. 244-358.

blending technologies, technology crossovers, and technologies pushing one another. Using this lens, the Second Industrial Revolution occurred between the last half of the nineteenth century and World War II. We will briefly review a few of the important innovations.

3.6.1 Electricity

Electricity has been known since the second millennium B.C. Electric fish, capable of stunning prey and predators, were described with fascination. Benjamin Franklin experimented with lightning. The phenomenon was known, but no one knew how to control it.

Experiments with batteries began in the late eighteenth century. Volta developed the zinc/copper battery in 1800, which quickly became the dominant design. In 1821, Faraday invented the electric motor, based on electromagnetism. Edison would apply the principle in reverse to invent the generator later in the century. Edison, after thousands of experiments, invented the electric light bulb, which displaced gas lighting. Westinghouse introduced the AC generator, which allowed transport of current over long distances. In the early twentieth century, electronic circuits were developed, incorporating components such as resistors, capacitors, transformers, and tubes. Electricity would serve as a critical component of other innovations, such as communications and transportation.

3.6.2 Communications

Experimenters in the early nineteenth century discovered that electrical pulses could be transmitted through a wire and detected at the other end. Samuel Morse developed the first recording telegraph in 1863, along with the code for its use. Over the next two decades, the Morse/Vail technology diffused across the United States. In 1861, it ran from coast to coast, consigning then the pony express to history.

In 1876, Alexander Graham Bell patented the telephone. Essentially, it was an improvement on the telegraph. Voice could be carried over a wire by modulating DC current. The first switchboard was introduced in Hungary later in the same year. Local exchanges were developed to direct calls from one user to another. National and international exchanges followed.

Herz and Tesla studied the transmission of radio waves in the early 1890s. In 1895, Marconi developed a radio transmitter capable of reaching several miles. He also formulated Marconi's Law, which stated that the range of the signal was proportional to the square of the height of the transmitter tower. Combining Morse code from the telegraph with the radio, Marconi commercialized the radio telegraph. This innovation enabled ship-to-ship and ship-to-shore communication. On shore, voice broadcasts began in the early 1900s in major cities. Entrepreneurs introduced commercial programming and sold commercial time. In a future era the portable two-way radio would morph into the cell phone.

3.6.3 Transportation

Animal powered transportation had been sufficient for several millennia, but it had its limitations. Animals had to be bred, fed, rested, and sheltered. Their speed and endurance were limited. Steam power had brought ships and railroads for mass transportation. Steam powered toy cars were demonstrated in China during the Ming dynasty. Steam powered automobiles appeared in the 19th century. They were inefficient and were outlawed in some states and cities.

In 1885, Karl Benz became the first commercial manufacturer of a petroleum powered automobile. By 1900, steam, electric, and petroleum powered cars were vying for attention. They began to push advances in other technologies. The petroleum industry began to distill and standardize fuels. Machinists developed gear drives and shift mechanisms. Materials were developed to pave roads. Henry Ford introduced the assembly line.

Since early times, man has observed the birds and envied their ability to defy gravity. Early experimenters fashioned wings and attempted to fly from peaks. Leonardo da Vinci drew diagrams of flying machines. In 1903, the Wright brothers became the first to fly a plane. World War I introduced air combat, using monoplanes and machine guns. The years 1918-1939 constitute the Golden Age of Aviation. Aviators barnstormed from city to city, displaying their talents and competing for records and prizes. Planes were becoming larger and more powerful. Body styles were being modified for better aerodynamics. Jimmy Doolittle invented flying by instruments. World War II would cause another wave of innovation in aircraft design.

3.6.4 Chemistry and Pharmaceuticals

Chemistry was not a new science. However, during the Second Industrial Revolution, it was advancing at a torrid pace. Germany was leading the pack. The Germans were so dominant that many universities required their chemistry majors to become skilled in reading the German reference books and journals. In Great Britain, Perkin discovered a reaction that produced mauve (1856), a useful synthetic dye[63]. British manufacturers had little core

---

[63] a) Landes, loc. cit., pp. 288-91, b) Cameron, loc. cit., p. 206.

competency producing dyes. By 1881, German producers had 50% of the world synthetic dye market. By 1900, their share was 90%. In 1875, Salvarsan, the first synthetic antibiotic, was observed to inhibit the growth of bacteria in the last part of the 19th century, but was not produced until 1928. Sulfa drugs were first introduced in the 1930s. Antibiotics were widely used in World War II.

3.6.5 Electronics and Communications

As a young boy, I remember turning on a radio that was larger than a 1980s console TV set. Inside were a dozen vacuum tubes, which could be pulled out and replaced when they burned out. Experiments with variable conductivity and theoretical advances in solid state physics led to the development of the semiconductor. After World War II, semiconductors were applied to transistors, amplifiers, and light emitting diodes (LED). The invention of integrated circuits kicked off a race toward miniaturization. More power could be packed into less space.

Computing aids have a long history, as exemplified by the abacus in Asia and the Middle East. In the 19th century, Herman Hollerith invented punch cards to store information. The first half of the 20th century saw the development of the mechanical calculator and the slide rule. The electronic computer became a commercial product. After World War I, early machines, such as the ENIAC and UNIVAC, were massive and power hungry. Replacement of vacuum tubes with solid state electronics dramatically improved efficiency. Machine language was augmented by a progressive development of higher level languages. Today we enjoy the advantages of mobile computing.

Telephone, radio, and audio have been discussed for their remarkable contributions to instantaneous communication. Each of these media improved through continuous innovation. Radical disruptive innovation occurred when these technologies were blended in novel ways. Television signals were delivered through wires and cable TV was born. Communication satellites enabled dish receivers, cell phones, and GPS. Tiny computers were added to create smart phones. Multiple computers are being networked to control functions in automobile, and the possibility of a self-driving car is being discussed. The internet grew out of the ARPA net project, designed to provide a redundant communication medium, in the event of a nuclear war. It grew into a gigantic library, business tool, and social medium.

3.7 Contemporary Innovations

Innovation exploded in a number of areas from World War II to the present. A number of names have been used, such as Information Age, Space Age, etc. We will explore a few areas that give a flavor of the frenetic pace. It has been an era of explosive growth, with some new industries being created and others falling into obsolescence.

3.7.1 The Space Race and Beyond

Wars are all about innovation. Consider the Marine Corps saying: "improvise, adapt, and overcome." The Cold War was no exception. The race to dominate beyond the confines of our planet is a vivid example.

Germany developed the V-1 and V-2 rockets to bombard and terrorize Great Britain. The Royal Air Force was powerless to stop them. When the war ended, the U. S. and the U. S. S. R.

recruited German aeronautical engineers and scientists to develop intercontinental ballistic missiles, tipped with nuclear warheads. In 1957, the Soviet Union shocked the world by launching Sputnik, the first continuous orbiting satellite. They followed with a manned flight; Yuri Gagarin became the first human to orbit the earth. The United States raced to catch up. In 1969, Neal Armstrong became the first man to walk on the moon. Construction began on the International Space Station, ensuring a permanent presence in space. Currently, private industry has begun to invest in extra-terrestrial projects.

Innovations that were necessary to achieve these milestones were extended to earthbound technologies. New composite materials were used in aircraft and many other products. Solar energy and battery technology were applied in computers, calculators, and other electronic products. Advances in medical monitoring and imaging were also spin-offs. Communications have been revolutionized. Of course, military applications remain. American, Russian, and Chinese satellites continue to orbit the earth, conducting surveillance and providing intelligence.

3.7.2 Financial Innovation

Banking and financial instruments date back to the Middle Ages. Promissory notes and letters of credit were used to facilitate trade. Stock companies were alternately created and banned in Europe, depending on who was in power. Systems of accounting were created to operate businesses and report financial results honestly. It became a very serious and straight-laced profession. An elderly business professor once said: "creativity is a trait you seek in R&D, but would be undesirable for your accountant." Nevertheless, where there is a demand, there will surely be an innovator, who will create a product to meet that demand.

Starting in the 1980s, banks, and mortgage companies began to feel dissatisfied with the returns on their investments. Many began to loosen their credit standards in order to collect higher interest payments. Savings and loan companies invested heavily in Texas real estate, which was fueled by resurgences in the oil industry. One humorous comment claimed that the state bird of Texas was the Crane. In the mid-1980s oil prices collapsed. Mass layoffs in the oil industry spread through the entire Texas economy. As a restaurant owner said when he closed his doors, "I never knew I was in the oil business!" S&Ls were left holding massive amounts of unsalable properties.

Globalization offered another opportunity to create innovative financial instruments. Global investors were seeking high yield investments in stable countries. Banks were dissatisfied with holding fixed interest mortgages for 30 years. Investment firms began to purchase mortgages, bundle them together, and sell them to investors. The collateralized debt obligation (CDO) was born. Banks were happy to churn funds to earn more income. Investors flocked to these new instruments. Insurance companies were making money by insuring CDOs. Everyone was so pleased that a shortage of CDOs developed. Sub-prime, interest-only, and negative-amortization loans were created to increase the supply of mortgages. Insufficient income verification resulted in "liar loans" being issued. When unqualified buyers began to default on their mortgages, the bubble burst. Speculators and flippers walked away from their obligations. It was the S&L crisis in a global scale, and the international markets started to collapse. After acrimonious debate, the United States government began a massive recapitalization of the largest banks. They were "too big to fail."

3.8 Lessons from History

A widely used expression is, "Insanity is trying the same thing over and over, and expecting a different result." I raise the question: "Is it really the same thing, and if so, was it just ahead of its time?" Thalidomide was sold in the 1950s as a sleeping pill, until pregnant women began to give birth to seriously deformed babies. Can you imagine the reaction of an R&D supervisor when, decades later, a scientist suggested, "maybe Thalidomide would be a good anticancer drug." This example illustrates both aspects of my question. Thalidomide today is not the same drug. In the 1950s, it was a 50:50 mixture of optical isomers, one therapeutic and the other a teratogen. The drug was ahead of its time because, in the 1950s, there was no process to separate optical isomers. So what can we learn from the historical narrative?

Innovation has three requirements: 1) A problem to solve; 2) A prepared mind; and 3) An available means to solve the problem. As discussed earlier, humans were limited in the Stone Age by a scarcity of enabling technologies. Today, innovations are so numerous and progress so rapidly that experts have trouble keeping up. There are many educated and trained minds and numerous technologies available. Innovations today are solving problems that we didn't even recognize a few decades ago. We are paying every month for innovations like internet, WI-FI, subscription TV and home security systems.

Innovation is a process that is subject to numerous invisible forces that can encourage, delay, or terminate it. In a favorable environment, one or more idea(s) are demonstrated. This sets off intense competition among innovators. In the early 20th century, there were hundreds of automobile manufacturers. Eventually, a handful of dominant designs emerge. Standardization begins to take shape. Marketing and finance skills, which were there from the early stages, take more dominant roles as the industry consolidates.

The financial crisis of 2008 is a reminder that not all innovations are universally beneficial. Additional examples are nuclear weapons, Africanized bees, and lead paint. Therefore, benefits must occasionally be compared to potential risks. Technology is also morally neutral. The same communications medium that allows cancer researchers to collaborate may also be used to disseminate child pornography. Unfortunately, poorly written regulations may have the unintended consequence of reducing benefits.

PART II

SEARCHING FOR THE PERFECT ECONOMIC SYSTEM

In Part I, we briefly reviewed the laws and ethics of the human race, the religious restrictions on business activity, and increasing rate of innovation as enabling technologies developed and were integrated.

Part II will compare economic systems, and briefly discuss their progression into blended economic practicality (Chapter 4). Chapter 5 will further dissect the core beliefs of the different systems and select the best features of each. Parts will then be assembled to produce the outline of a new traditional economy.

Chapter 4

Comparative Economics

"Capitalism is the legitimate racket of the ruling class."
-Al Capone-

"…the inherent virtue of socialism is the
equal sharing of miseries."
-Winston Churchill-

4.1 Introduction

Throughout history, economic resources and markets have been managed by tribes, religious groups, and governments. The systems have ranged from laissez-faire capitalism to true communism. Politicians have extolled the virtues of both extremes, inspiring the academic discipline of political economy. Rosser and Rosser have reviewed the area in detail[64]. The recent economic growth of China appears to have arisen from a hybrid

---

[64] J. B. Rosser and M. V. Rosser, *Comparative Economics in a Transforming World Economy*, MIT Press (2003).

system, termed state capitalism. For the purposes of this book, the main features of the various systems will be briefly described. In the next chapter, I will attempt to digest the material from this and the preceding chapters, and resynthesize them into an economic system that can optimize all the diverse aspirations of humanity.

Four major characteristics determine the nature of a political economy. Ownership may be private or held in common by the state. Economic decisions are made by business owners or by government central planners. Income distribution may be even or uneven. Governments may be dictators or liberal democracies. Note that "liberal" is used in its original meaning "free," not in its contemporary usage of liberal versus conservative. Of course, in any social, political, or economic system, numerous other factors may exert important influences.

From ancient times, land and assets were privately owned. The strong held their own and often seized the assets of the weak. As societies formed, laws and customs were established to encourage cohesiveness. However, two areas are still frequently disputed. Common properties, such as rivers and lakes have been the cause of many disputes. In the last few years, there have been disagreements over water use in California, Florida, and Georgia, as well as protests over the vast amounts of land owned by the U.S. government. Free goods, such as seafood and game, are difficult problems to manage[65]. Businesses have been traditionally owned by individuals and groups. Private ownership is a major attribute of capitalism. Common ownership was a tenant of Karl Marx's Communist Manifesto, and is a key defining factor of Socialism. Many recent economies have had mixtures of both public and private ownership. For example, businesses are privately owned, while public utilities may be owned by the government.

---

[65] Commercial fishermen strongly disagree that fish are free.

Planning and decision making are generally made by the owners of productive assets. In a capitalist system, business owners plan and implement their own strategies. A basic tenet of Socialism is that economic activity would be centrally planned. History, as it often does, has provided exceptions to these rules. Adolph Hitler retained private ownership under the Third Reich, but imposed rigid government planning. The United States did the same during World War II. Recently, China has decentralized some of its planning functions, while maintaining its Socialist economic structure.

Distribution of income is an important characteristic of political economic systems. After paying expenses, economic outputs are distributed as wages and profits. Profits may be further allocated to bonuses, dividends, and reinvestment. Capitalist systems treat wages as the cost of labor. Sole proprietors take a portion of their profit as income. Karl Marx expropriated the Bible verse, "from each according to their ability, to each according to their need," as the basis for equitable distribution. Unfortunately, real Marxist governments were never able to achieve this ideal.

There is not as high a degree of correlation between government type and political economy as there is with other factors. Dictatorships may have either Capitalist or Socialist economies. Liberal democracies may have significant government controls on their economic activities. The strong rule of a dictator is usually associated with a lack of personal and economic freedom. If the economy is centrally planned, the consumer has little input as to which goods are produced. This may account for the proliferation of western goods finding their way into the Soviet Union during the Cold War. Advocates for dictatorship (there are a few) stress the efficiency of simple decisions. They also suggest that a benevolent dictator could be an effective leader. Landes has described such a person[66]. Dr. Casper Rodriguez de Francia was a dictator in Paraguay in the early 19th century. The population was predominantly Guaraní Indian. He was a strong leader, committed to carrying out the popular will through his edicts. An Indian sharecropper was treated with more respect than a land owner. His sons carried on in this tradition. Their reign came to an end in 1867, when neighboring countries waged a three-year war against Paraguay. Both men and women fought gallantly for their beloved dictator.

4.2 Economic Systems

Political economies can be categorized according to ownership and control of the factors of production. In an agricultural economy, the factors are land, capital, and labor. In an industrial economy, land is replaced by resources, which are inputs to industries. Examples of inputs are raw materials, physical plant, and energy. At the ends of the scale are capitalism and socialism. Pure forms of these systems are rare today, and most economies have modified elements of both. Another type of system making resurgence is the new traditional economy.

4.3 Capitalism[67]

Historians associate the beginning of capitalism with the collapse of the manorial system in the 14th century. Famines and the Black Death reduced the population of Europe, resulting in an end of serf labor. Although mercantilism had existed for a few millennia, mercantile capitalism was established. Amsterdam was the epicenter. In the 16th century, the Netherland, Spain, France,

---

[66] Landes, loc. cit., pp. 329-334.
[67] a) "History of Capitalism," http://www.wikipedia.com; b) Rosser, loc. cit., pp. 23-52.

Portugal, and Great Britain utilized colonialism to spread the capitalist system across the globe. The Industrial Revolution shifted the global economy toward mass production. Material inputs were still derived from agriculture and mining. In the mid-19th century, centralized banking was established in Britain. When paper currency was issued by the government, it was backed by a store of precious metals in a central location. Other countries followed suit, providing ready capital for industrial ventures. Although slave labor was disappearing, unskilled labor was abundant and therefore paid very low wages.

Laissez-faire capitalism was characterized by private ownership, little government intervention, and competition to meet demands of the customers. This system, in theory, allocated scarce resources efficiently. Innovators look at the problem of scarce resources differently, but that point will be discussed in Chapter 5. Perfect markets were pictured as producing the exact quantity needed to satisfy demand (Pareto optimum). Complete information should be available to all buyers and sellers. A large number of buyers and sellers would ensure a competitive free market. Of course, in a real economy, this level of ideality is not easily achievable. At static Pareto optimality, no one can become better off without someone else becoming worse off. Fortunately, real economic systems are capable of dynamic growth.

Where there are many perfectly-informed buyers and sellers in a market, and there are low barriers to entry and exit, a condition of pure competition exists. When the number of buyers and/or sellers is reduced, competition may become less ideal. At the extreme, all the wealth and power may be concentrated in a single entity. This situation constitutes a monopoly[68]. In microeconomic theory, supply is reduced and prices are higher in a monopoly than in a competitive market. This is because firms in a competitive market

---

[68] Rosser, loc. cit., pp. 25-31.

will produce until the marginal cost (the cost of producing one more unit) is equal to the marginal revenue. A monopolist will produce until the average total cost is equal to the marginal revenue. In most cases, the average total cost is lower; fewer units are produced by a monopolist. Theodore Roosevelt recognized the adverse effect on the economy. The United States enacted the Sherman and Clayton anti-trust laws at the end of the 19th century. In some cases monopolies are the most practical market structure. For example, public utilities may be operated as monopolies under state control.

Between pure competition and monopoly, there is a case where several firms control a large share of a particular market. This could pose a problem if these firms collude to fix prices or restrict supply of the product. One example is the Organization of Petroleum Exporting Countries (OPEC), a cartel. OPEC meets periodically to set production quotas for the member countries. When supply is lowered relative to demand, prices rise and cartel members reap higher profits. Cartels are only effective if their members control enough supply, and if the members faithfully adhere to their quotas. OPEC had problems with countries cheating on their quotas.

Most capitalist economies operate in a free market, except during times of war as previously mentioned. Most market capitalist countries have democratic governments. Prominent exceptions are Hong Kong and Singapore, now governed by the People's Republic of China. Many governments influence firms' conduct through tax policy and regulations. These policies can vary from one country to another. New Zealand has low corporate taxes and loose restrictions. France has higher taxes and tighter regulations.

4.4 Socialism[69]

The early concepts of socialism were proposed by British and French social critics such as Robert Owen, Charles Fourier, and Saint Simon. They condemned the unequal distribution created by the Industrial Revolution. Their vision was to establish small communities where private property would be abolished and wealth would be divided evenly. Their vision was called Utopia. In 1848, Karl Marx and Frederick Engels published the Communist Manifesto, which called for a violent revolution by the working class (proletariat) against the bourgeois property owners. A dictatorship of the proletariat was seen by Marx as a transitional stage toward an ideal society where there was no class conflict. Competing socialist agendas arose throughout the world. Social democratic parties wanted a more gradual path to communism. Some even favored preserving the capitalist structure. Marx and Engels labeled them revisionists. Anarchists believed in overthrowing capitalism and redistribution of wealth, but rejected the need for a formal govern apparatus.

Marx redefined the factors of production in terms of labor hours expended. In other words, Marx considered capital, land, and resources were stolen from workers by the bourgeois capital class. While residing in Britain, Marx developed the formal equations to support his theory[70]

In the political arena, socialists established and supported trade unions. In Europe, Australia, New Zealand, and parts of Canada, socialist parties began to win elections. In October 1917, Bolsheviks seized power in Russia, under the leadership of Vladimir Lenin and Leon Trotsky. Following the death of Lenin,

---

[69] a) "History of Socialism," http://www.wikipedia.com; b) Rosser, loc. cit., pp. 53-84.
[70] Rossser, loc. cit., pp. 57-60.

Josef Stalin seized power and established a strong centralized government with rigid economic planning authority (Command Socialism). His methods were brutal, resulting in numerous deaths. Following World War II, The Soviets became involved in the Cold War against the United States and its allies. Following a series of attempts to reform, the Soviet alliance fell apart in the early 1990s. China was more successful implementing a shift to a Market Socialist economy, following the death of Mao Tse-tung and the overthrow of the Red Guard.

Progressive advocates of capitalism sought ways to avoid the class struggle described by Marx. Worker participation in ownership and/or management seemed to be a logical approach to reduce confrontation and labor unrest. Cooperatives can be owned and operated by workers. For example, some plywood manufacturers in the northwest United States are owned and operated by the workers[71]. As owners, the workers are fully exposed to economic risk. Profit sharing and employee stock ownership plans are vehicles to improve the distribution of wealth. The Anderson Clayton Company had a profit sharing plan which distributed stock to employees based on the employee's salary, performance rating, and the net income of the company. The stock was only distributed when the employee retired or left the company. After an intense bidding war, the company was taken over by Quaker Oats in 1986. Following the takeover many long-time employees lost their jobs, but were cushioned by distribution of Anderson Clayton stock at an enormously inflated price[72].

An entrepreneur once said: "the best way to beat a capitalist is to become one!" Entrepreneurship has a lot in common with a cooperative. An individual owner bears the economic risk. He or

---

[71] Ibid., p. 74.
[72] Author's first person experience.

she has no one else to blame if the business fails. Some people are just not comfortable working for someone else. They may feel exploited or feel they have better ideas of how a business should be run. Large companies have recently found it more economical to retain an independent contractor than to hire a full-time employee. This is particularly true in a "feast or famine" business. Entrepreneurs tend to be innovative and impulsive risk takers. They often form new businesses where large conservative companies don't want to assume the risk.

4.5 New Traditional Economies[73]

So far, we have discussed economies as a separate system, governed by the civil laws of individual countries. This has not always been the case. Historically, some economic systems were embedded in and subservient to religious authority. Judaic law regulated merchants' behavior in ancient Israel. Chinese dynasties controlled businesses according to the principles of Confucius. Mohammed was a merchant in his early life, so the Koran has numerous examples regarding commerce. Some large countries are revisiting these ideas. Rosser describes this as New Traditionalism.

Islamic law governs personal and social behavior in much of the Middle East, some former Soviet republics, and Malaysia. Sharia law is interpreted differently among the various Muslim traditions[74]. The major distinction is between the Sunni and Shiite sects. Islamic economics is built on three principles: 1) *Tawhd* (divine unity) means that all economic activity must be in accord with divine commands; 2) *Viceregency* (universal brotherhood) is the idea that humans are partners with Allah in managing the

---

[73] Rosser, loc. cit., pp. 85-112.
[74] Ibid., p. 100.

world; 3) *Adalah* (justice) is a concern for the welfare of others. Saudi Arabia exerts a great deal of influence in the Sunni tradition, while Iran is emblematic of the Shiite economic vision[75].

Buddhist economics can be fitted into either a capitalist system, as seen in Thailand, or socialism, which existed in Myanmar (Burma). Confucian economics concentrates on order, harmony, and a system of hierarchy. The economy is supervised by educated elite, but market forces can also play a role. Hindu economic theory is based on the efficiency of the division of labor. Mahatma Gandhi reformed the caste system and implemented the self-sufficiency of villages. The Indian economy has been one of the fastest growing in the 21st century.

4.6 Summary

Ancient history describes the evolution of economic activity from hunter-gatherer through mercantilism. Kings and emperors were in charge. The Industrial Revolution spawned the capitalist economic system. The system stimulated many inventions which improved standards of living. Unfortunately, wealth became concentrated among wealthy capitalists. Utopian and socialist thought grew in reaction to the exploitive characteristics of capitalism. The Russian Revolution led to the creation of the Soviet Union. Most of these countries had command socialist economies, lacking personal, political, and consumer freedom. The collapse of the Soviet Union was followed by migration back toward capitalist or market socialist economies. New Traditional economies began to take shape in the Middle East and Asia, starting in the last half of the 20th century.

---

[75] Ibid., pp. 487-514.

Chapter 5

Why Compassionate Capitalism?

"Business will migrate to where it is best treated."
-Confucius-

"You can't mandate what's not in people's hearts."
-Dr. Robert Avossa, Superintendent of Palm Beach Schools-

5.1 Introduction

Rondo Cameron asked an intriguing question. Is it better to have a wealthy economy with uneven distribution of wealth or a slightly poorer economy where wealth is more evenly distributed? The only problem with this question is that it is examining static conditions. In a dynamic context, the question would become: Is it better to have a growing economy where wealth is unevenly distributed or a stagnant economy where wealth is more evenly distributed? The answer to this hypothetical riddle is, like most of life's problems, it depends! If the population in our hypothetical case is growing, is the per capita income rising or falling? The qualifying question becomes: Is the system fair? Does everyone have an opportunity to gain wealth? In this section, we will make an attempt to propose such a system.

5.2 Why is Economic Growth Essential?

At Pareto equilibrium, the amount produced is exactly equal to the amount consumed. This is an economist's vision of perfect efficiency. No one can become better off without making someone else's situation worse. An average person would not perceive this an ideal situation. It would be like jogging in place. Prices would be constant as long as the supply matches demand. As the population grows, production must increase to match demand. If supply does not keep up, everyone becomes worse off. To measure this for a particular country, one would calculate per capita income, per capita Gross Domestic Product, and per capita growth in these two categories. Of course, this is only a starting point, since these statistics are only averages and give no guidance as to how the income is distributed. Charts that break the status down by income groups would be more informative, particularly for growth (GDP). Economic growth could be considered successful if all income groups were moving in a positive direction.

When a ruler asked what he should do for his people, Confucius advised him to make them wealthy and to educate them. These Confucian principles suggest that growing wealth makes people materially happy, while education provides mental and spiritual satisfaction. The ideal economy from a human perspective would promote growth of per capita income and per capita GDP.

So how do we achieve economic growth? History suggests that the rocket fuel for growth is innovation. It is a function of the number of technologies available to solve problems. Acemoglu, in his excellent book on economic growth models, was so convinced of the importance of technology that he devoted four chapters to it[76] as we have seen in Chapter 3; the Stone Age lasted millions of years because of the lack of enabling technologies. The 20th century demonstrated explosive, all but uneven, growth because of applications of technologies to create new products and services. However, innovation, like other processes, is subject to a number of invisible forces. It's critical to identify these forces, and navigate them to be successful.

5.3 Creative Destruction vs. Preservation

Joseph Schumpeter was the first to describe innovation as the destruction of current products and services[77]. However, not all faces of innovation are destructive. Tushman and Anderson described four types of innovations and their organizational technical and marketing competencies[78]:

Incremental innovation preserves both technical and marketing competencies. Productivity and quality improvement are examples.

Niche marketing preserves technical but disrupts marketing competencies. Improving quality of a mature product and selling into a specialized market can improve a company's profits. For example, a delivery system for a drug.

[76] D. Acemoglu, *Introduction to Modern Economic Growth*, Princeton University Press, 2009, Chapters 12-16.
[77] T. K. See and M. McCrey, *Prophet of Innovation: Joseph Schumpeter and Creative Destruction*, Belknap Press, 2010.
[78] a) M. L. Tushman and P. Anderson, "Technological Discontinuities and Organizational Environments," Administrative Science Quarterly, (31), 1986, pp. 439-65, b) P. Anderson and M. Tushman, "Technological Discontinuities and Dominant Designs," Administrative Science Quarterly, (35), 1990, pp. 604-33.

Gerard L. Hasenhuettl

Radical innovation preserves marketing, but disrupts technical competencies. Transistors were sold by many of the sales channels that sold vacuum tubes.

Architectural innovation destroys both technical and marketing competencies. A new dominant design will transform a mature industry or an entirely new industry may be created.

Mature industries that are disrupted do not go quietly. They may engage in a frenzied effort to improve their own products and services. After Edison invented the electric light bulb, gas lighting companies introduced the Weisbach mantle to improve the brightness of the flames, yielding more lumens per volume of gas[79]. Utterback has described how leading companies have been displaced by waves of innovation in industries such as ice harvesting[80], photography[81], and incandescent lighting[82]. In his book, *The Innovator's Dilemma*, Christensen drew a distinction between supporting and disruptive innovations[83]. He points out that well-managed companies adapt very well to supporting technologies. However, the conventional tools of management, such as listening to the customer and resource allocation, cause these companies to miss disruptive shifts in new technologies. Today, modern firms attempt to build disruptive design into their strategic planning process.

---

[79] J. M. Utterback, *Mastering the Dynamics of Innovation: How Companies Can Seize Opportunities in the Face of Technological Change*, Harvard Business School Press, 1994, pp. 65, 74
[80] Ibid., pp. 146-57.
[81] Ibid., pp. 167-186.
[82] Ibid., pp. 62-86.
[83] C. M. Christensen, *The Innovator's Dilemma: When New Technologies Cause Great Firms to Fail*, Harvard Business School Press, 1997.

Jeff Dyer and co-workers described five skills that are critical for innovators[84]. Associating is the ability to link together ideas from dissimilar disciplines. Questioning allows the innovator to challenge aspects of the current process or product. Observing is a useful skill that is complementary to questioning. Networking is essential wherever an unfamiliar technology may fit into a product or process. Experimenting is necessary to evaluate a new idea. Perhaps the most prolific experimenter was Thomas Edison. Experiments may be exploratory to evaluate feasibility or optimization to set the best design and operating conditions. In the latter case, statistical design skills are very useful. The second part of Dyer's book focuses on disruptive organizations and their leaders.

Innovation for entrepreneurs is a bottom-up process, as shown in Figure 5.1. In the 1980's many successful businesses were started in garages, basements, and dorm rooms, resulting in large corporations like Apple, Microsoft, and Dell. The foundation is laid when an idea is born, and then refined by reading and collaborating with colleagues. The next level is experimentation, which proves the feasibility of the idea. At the completion, the invention qualifies for patent consideration. Implementation or manufacturing results in a standardization of the new product or process. Although marketing and distribution is the final stage, it is generally planned from the foundation phase. The innovation process for the idea is never finished. Continuous improvement and surveillance for the next disruption must be continued.

---

[84] J. Dyer et al., *The Innovators DNA: Mastering the Five Skills of Disruptive Innovation*, Harvard Business Review Press, 2011, pp. 17-256.

Gerard L. Hasenhuettl

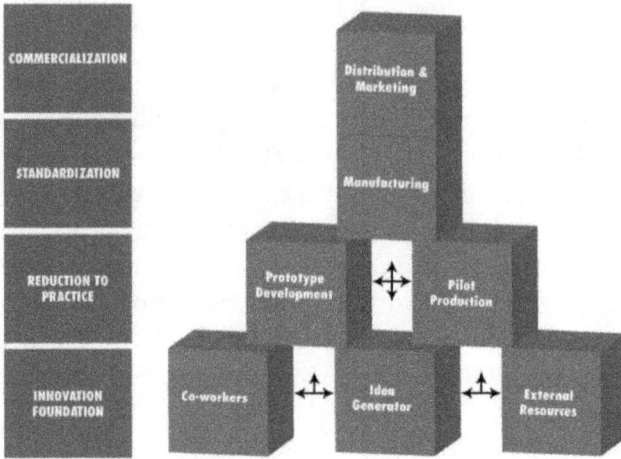

Figure 5.1 An Entrepreneur's View of Innovation

An Entrepreneur's View of Innovation

Once an innovative product or service has been launched, the life cycle begins to run. As shown in Figure 5.2, the product begins to descend a waterfall toward a run-of-the-mill commodity. Standardization increases and skills required for implementation become more routine. The deterioration of the innovative status also serves to fuel globalization. Aging products are handed off to developing economies, and then to less developed countries. The aging process can be slowed by use of patents, copyrights, and trademarks (intellectual property), but the process will grind on.

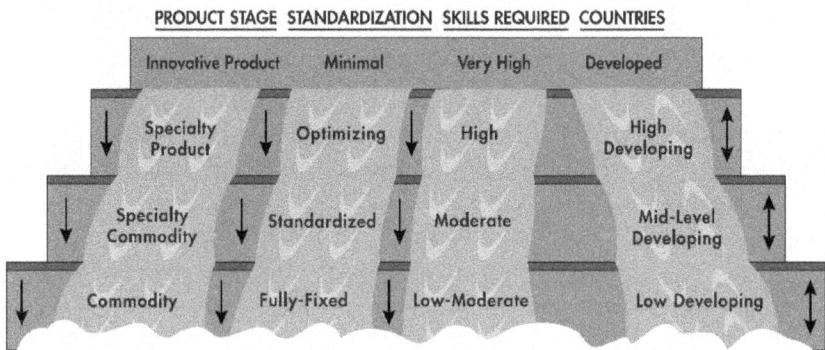

PRODUCT STAGE	STANDARDIZATION	SKILLS REQUIRED	COUNTRIES
Innovative Product	Minimal	Very High	Developed
Specialty Product	Optimizing	High	High Developing
Specialty Commodity	Standardized	Moderate	Mid-Level Developing
Commodity	Fully-Fixed	Low-Moderate	Low Developing

Life Cycle of an Innovative Product

Countries are forced to swim up the waterfall like salmon to prevent being swept to the bottom of the economic order. This effort is beneficial in the educational and personal development of the population. The Bloomberg Innovation Index rated the countries of the world, using such criteria as R&D spending, concentration on high technology, advanced degrees in math and sciences, value-added manufacturing and patent activity[85]. South Korea captured the top ranking, followed by Germany, Sweden, Japan, and Switzerland. Tunisia leads in the number of advanced technical degrees, but was lacking in the other criteria. The result is a large number of highly-educated people without jobs, another example of the law of supply and demand.

Freedom may be a critical, but often overlooked, factor that affects innovation and subsequent economic growth. Table 5.1 summarizes ranking and rating of economic, personal, and press freedom for the top five and bottom five countries. A cursory examination indicates that the top five economically-free countries have vibrant economies, while the bottom five have lower standards of living. This observation may be biased by the fact North Korea and Cuba have been under trade sanctions. Another exception is oil-producing countries that have high per capita GDP's, but are under religious restrictions that limit some freedoms. On an individual level, personal and economic freedom enables innovators to pursue their visions.

---

[85] M. Jamrisko and w. Lu, *These Are the World's Most Innovative Economies,* *http://*www.bloomberg.com/news/articles/2016_01_19/these_are_the_worlds_ most_innovative_economies.

Table 5.1 Freedom Rankings for Top and Bottom Countries

Country	Economic Freedom* Rank/Score/Trend	Personal Freedom** Rank/Score (1-10)	Press Freedom*** Rank/Index
Hong Kong	1/86.8/1.0	1/9.08	69/28.50
Singapore	2/87.8/-1.6	43/7.05	154/52.96
New Zealand	3/81.6/-0.5	5/8.97	5/10.01
Switzerland	4/81.0/+0.5	2/9.40	7/11.76
Australia	5/80.3/-1.1	7/9.23	25/17.84
United States	11/75.1/-0.8	20/8.26	41/22.49
Turkmenistan	174/41.9/+0.5	108/6.14	178/83.44
Zimbabwe	175/38.2/+0.6	149/4.59	124/40.41
Venezuela	176/33.7/-0.6	144/6.59	139/44.77
Cuba	177/29.8/+0.2	Not Rated	171/70.23
North Korea	178/2.3/1.0	Not Rated	179/83.76

*Data from The Heritage Foundation Ranking on Economic Freedom, http://www.heritage.org/index/ranking.
**Data from Cato Institute's 2012 Human Freedom Index, www.cato.org/human_freedom_index.
***Data from Reporters Without Borders Press Freedom Ranking – 2016, http://www.rsf.org/en/ranking_table.

5.4 Command vs. Free Market Economy

Command economies have had less than spectacular records in recent history. This may be due to a conflict of two basic human instincts. The first is the compulsive need to tell other people what to do. The opposing instinct is to have the freedom to make one's own choices. In a command economy, freedom has been taken from the consumer and given to a central planning authority. Consumers may resist in many ways, including accession to the black market to find the products and services they prefer. American designer jeans, western music, and entertainment were wildly popular in Iron Curtain countries.

A central principle of physics states: "for every action, there is an equal and opposite reaction." Perhaps there is a similar natural law governing human behavior (see Appendix B). Before the fall of the Iron Curtain, approximately 95% of the population in Poland was Catholic. Was this an overt opposition to the despotic government of the Soviet Union? When President Obama proposed tightening restrictions on gun purchases, gun stores were packed as people scrambled to horde weapons. Classes for concealed carry permits were packed beyond capacity. Freedom was rebelling against authoritarianism. Some resistance may not even be visible, but may be manifested by passive-aggressive behavior. Some may ignore the efforts of government authorities, regarding them as irrelevant to their daily lives.

The most devastating weakness of the command economy is that it is incompatible with innovation. Part of incremental innovation is the continuous increase in productivity. Fewer people are required to produce the same quantity of product. Alternatively, more products may be produced with the same number of people. This is contrary to the goals of governments and trade unions, who want to preserve and create jobs. The end result can be described by the Russian saying: "We pretend to work and they pretend to pay us." When a global corporation bought out a manufacturing plant in Poland, it laid off one-third of the employees who had no useful functions.

After 25 years of experience with companies of various sizes, I formulated Jerry's First Law of Innovation, which states: "radical and architectural innovations are unwelcome in large organizations." This is actually a very obvious statement. Large organizations have made large investments in current technology, plants, equipment, and distribution channels. They would not be receptive to an idea that would render it all obsolete. Small companies and those outside the industry have no such investments. Christensen and Utterback found that many, if not most, disruptive innovations were initiated by firms outside the industry.

In a command economy, the government is the ultimate large organization. Its planning authority employs "experts" to decide which projects to accept or reject. Often, these experts are chosen because of their political connections, rather than their knowledge of the field. Even if they are knowledgeable, they may have prejudices that may obstruct new ideas. During the Cold War, the Romanian National Ministry of Science and Technology was headed by Elena Polrescu, wife of President Nicolae Ceausescu[86]. Even prolific innovators can reverse course and become obstructionists. Thomas Edison, probably the world's most prolific inventor, did everything he could to obstruct the Westinghouse AC generator, because it would displace the DC generator that Edison had invented for electric power transmission[87].

Iron Curtain countries are examples of what can befall command socialist economies. After 1992, the countries have been reforming their economies, with varying strategies and degrees of success. Studying the results of these programs could provide valuable information to countries planning to make this transition. Centrally-planned capitalist economies can also fail to acknowledge disruptive change. Even though nuclear fission was

---

[86] http://www.ceausescu.org/ceausescu_texts/elena_ceausescus_cult.html.
[87] Utterback, loc. cit., pp. 74-5.

95

discovered in Germany, the Third Reich never initiated a program to develop a nuclear weapon. One can only imagine what would have happened if they had done so.

The obvious question is: if command economies are so dysfunctional, why would anyone want to live in one? Some environmentalists point out that free market economies produce more product than needed to meet demand. This is a result of multiple brands, competing for attention. Environmentalists claim this wastes raw materials and energy. Possible solutions to this problem are secondary markets and more efficient recycling methods.

People with no or few marketable skills cling to command economies that support their basic needs. This need is supported with the Judaic concept of the "valueless value," previously discussed in Chapter 2. Capitalist economies have dealt with this issue by initiating welfare, unemployment, and job retraining programs.

5.5 Capitalism vs. Socialism

A head-to-head comparison of capitalism and socialism is not a straightforward task. Different countries have a diversity of social, political, and religious traditions. For example, Asian countries have long histories of autocratic rule. Individuals have subordinated their ambitions to the goals of the state. Western countries are more accustomed to participatory democracy. As Landes has pointed out, factors, such as climate and natural resources, impact national wealth[88]. In practice, capitalism and socialism have strayed from pure theory. Marx predicted that the

---

[88] Landes, loc. cit.

"dictatorship of the proletariat" would be a temporary phase. For the Soviet Union, it was about 75 years, from beginning to end.

A preliminary look at results would suggest that economic growth has been greater in countries with capitalist economies. Even Robin Hahnel, a strong proponent of socialism, concedes that capitalism is "energetic." However, 20th century socialism has been associated with a command economic system in the overwhelming[89] majority of cases. Modern socialism has been moving toward the free market system. Olaf Gersemann has presented an extensive comparison of U. S. capitalism with France, Germany, and Italy during the period 1992-2002, when these countries had socialist governments[90]. Data for unemployment, per capita income, and hours worked, R&D spending, high-tech production, and wages were compared and generally showed better results for American capitalism. Currently, comparisons are being made for the economic status of the U. S. and the European Economic Community.

In the second half of the 20th century, China made sharp turns into the Cultural Revolution, and then back to a reform movement, which steered the economy back toward a focus on markets. However, the structure of the government remained autocratic. In recent years, China has experienced rapid, double-digit economic growth. Chow has attributed much of this growth to the decentralization of economic planning.[91] China has also developed a robust export economy, by leveraging its large labor force. Companies from highly industrialized countries outsourced their manufacturing to China to lower their costs. Creative adjustments to the currency have also enhanced the Chinese competitive

---

[89] Hahnel, loc. cit.
[90] O. Gersemann, *Cowboy Capitalism: European Myth, American Reality*, Cato Institute, 2005.
[91] G. C. Chow, *China's Economic Transformation*, 2nd Ed., Wiley/Blackwell Publishers, 2002.

position. A key question is whether China can continue to grow enough to alleviate its global poverty.

Hahnel has proposed an interesting worker-managed socialist system, which he describes as libertarian socialism[92]. A bottom-up planning approach would focus on how many units would be produced at each plant. Planning at the national level would consist of mere consolidation. Hahnel solves the free rider problem, seen in previous socialist regimes, with peer review, based on effort rather than results. There is sparse precedent for such a system. Perhaps the closest analogy was the worker-managed economy in communist Yugoslavia[93]. This economy displayed good growth for several years, but then disintegrated. Other factors, such as ethnic conflict, may have played a role, so lessons from Yugoslavia might be flawed.

A major concern about libertarian socialism is how they would implement innovation, particularly disruptive innovation. Workers are valuable resources for incremental innovation. Would they be willing to invest part of their budget to something radically different? If not, would an outside group be empowered to develop it? It would be interesting to see a test of this system in a small country, or a region of a larger country. In a free economy, a believer in libertarian socialism would be able to found a company and operate it based on the principles of libertarian socialism.

After the break-up of Yugoslavia, Slovenia began a transition toward privatization and a market economy[94]. The country took a gradual approach and allowed worker groups to purchase assets. Government-owned, worker-owned, and privately-owned

---

[92] Hahnel, loc. cit.
[93] Rosser, loc. cit., pp. 387-416.
[94] Ibid., pp. 409-416.

enterprises co-existed. Slovenia was so successful that it was the first of the former Yugoslav republics admitted to the European Economic Community. It is tempting to speculate whether competition with privately-owned firms made worker-owned companies better. It may be an example of worker-owned capitalism. In the United States, some companies have reorganized from bankruptcy by ceding shares of the company to their workers.

5.6 The Proposal for Compassionate Capitalism

For the past few centuries, capitalism has had the most consistent record of nourishing innovation to promote economic growth. We need this system to generate income and GDP growth to improve everyone's lives. The nation's government needs to provide an encouraging, but not controlling environment for innovation and growth. Financial and venture capital groups should be willing to invest in new businesses.

There are two major problems entangled in the capitalist economic system. The first is that profits and income are unevenly distributed; the second is the boom/bust business cycle. Corruption is a major problem, but it is not unique to capitalism. The boom/bust cycle is due to excessive risk and poor decision making on a group think level. This can be managed by insurance and leverage limits. Uneven wealth distribution is something that people will accept if they believe the system is fair. So how do we make capitalism more compassionate? It can be done by weaving a new traditional economy from the threads of diverse religious and humanist traditions. Essential prerequisites are commitment to integrity and freedom for all participants in the economy. All businesses and individuals should commit to the following:

- All people have the right to develop to their maximum potential (Humanism).

- Priority should be given to assisting the poor (Liberation Theology).

- Establish a strong work ethic (Protestantism).

- Displace envy with opportunity (Islam, Christianity, and Judaism).

5.6.1 Individual Development

Perhaps the most powerful driver of wealth and income inequality is the uneven development of individuals. A combination of education, experience, creativity, and sound judgment are necessary to succeed in a capitalist economy. Unfortunately, not everyone has an equal opportunity to develop these access keys. Poverty is one factor, but it is one which is possible to overcome. There are many anecdotes about individuals who started out poor, but studied and worked hard to become successful. There are probably many less inspiring stories about spoiled rich kids, who made bad decisions and fell to the bottom.

Education is one area, which is nominally equal in the United States, due to availability of public education. However, the results have been anything but equal. Until recent years, the system has been a rigid "one size fits all" model. Students attended lectures, read books, and wrote reports. Those who were unable to keep up were considered slow, unmotivated, or lacking intelligence. In the last two decades of the 20th century, education researchers discovered that individuals had unique learning styles[95]. While many learned well in the traditional academic style, many were kinesthetic or hands-on learners. Others were better suited to auditory, visual, or interactive experiences. Students also tend to learn subjects in which they are interested. Teachers can now work with students to individualize the learning experience. The concept, if not the methodology, of "no child left behind" should be embraced.

Another critical issue to confront is the digital divide. Intense efforts are under-way to bring better education to the masses at a dramatically-reduced cost. CNBC recently ran a week-long series on this subject[96]. However, these approaches require access to a computer and the internet. These are not always available in poor neighborhoods. Internet access is a monthly expense and computers are an attractive target for theft. School and library computers always seem to be crowded; one may have to sign up for a 30-minute session hours in advance.

Role models and mentors are often instrumental to personal and career development. In poverty-stricken communities, role models are present, but are easily overlooked. They quietly work hard and sacrifice to provide a better life for their families. Unfortunately, gang leaders and drug dealers grab the spotlight. Mentors come in all shapes and sizes. They are teachers, clergy, and neighbors that step up to help vulnerable children overcome obstacles to success.

5.6.2 Priority for the Poor

All three Middle East religions have strong traditions to care for the poor. This is achieved by directly giving assistance to the person or tithes given to their faith to care for the poor. According

---

[93] For example see S. Segal and D. Horne, *Human Dynamics*, Pegasus Communications Inc., Waltham, MA, 1997.
[96] Squawk Box, CNBC, December 2-6, 2013.

to Marxist class analysis, the bourgeois were rich capitalist exploiters and the proletariats were the working poor. That may have had some validity at the time, but today, the situation is more complex. Neither the rich nor the poor are monolithic classes. The rich could have attained their assets by inheritance, fraud or theft, or diligent hard work and sacrifice. The poor are in their situation voluntarily or involuntarily. Some people of faith volunteer to be poor in order to focus on spirituality. Others are content to live a simple lifestyle. Many are poor because of poor choices they make or continue to make. The involuntary poor may be sick or disabled. Children of the poor have not chosen their lot in life.

Helping voluntary poor who are addicted to drugs and alcohol is a problem, if that help allows the addict to continue to make poor choices. Not only is the person continuing to harm himself and his/her family, resources are being wasted. However, once the person decides to be sober, he becomes involuntarily poor. Recovering addicts can go on to lead productive lives, and even help others.

Another contribution of Liberation Theology is the formation of ecclesial communities. The poor cooperate to help other poor, especially if they have needed skills. Survivors of the Great Depression told stories of newly-poor neighbors, who bartered goods and services in an environment where money was scarce. Citizens also cooperated to reduce crime and maintain cleanliness in the neighborhood.

One measure of the strength of the United States has been the influx of immigrants seeking a better life. Many arrived with nothing and sought out neighborhoods of others who had come from the same country. Neighbors helped one another find jobs, learn English, and acclimate to the culture of their adopted country. Often, the new immigrants were part of a sacrificial generation. They worked multiple jobs to give their children the education that would allow them to become successful. Following the financial crisis of 2008, many families have had to start over and become the new sacrificial generation.

5.6.3 Promoting a Work Ethic

Starting around the 1950's, men and women who had experienced the Great Depression were raising children. They were diligent about providing food, clothing, shelter, and education. They did not spend lavishly on toys or recreation. Children got the message, that if they wanted that electric train, they would have to raise the money themselves. Many kids began mowing lawns, shoveling snow, or delivering newspapers. In addition to learning the value of money, they got experience in entrepreneurship, sales, and quality improvement.

In today's suburban neighborhoods, parents are more willing to provide their children with more non-essentials. They prefer to have their children focus on academics and sports. In poor neighborhoods, safety has become a major issue. It does little good to make money if you are consistently robbed. What is needed are community-based activities where children can safely earn spending money, while learning skills that will help them succeed as adults.

5.6.4 Emphasis on Opportunity

"Thou shalt not envy thy neighbor's goods (Exod. 20:17)," is one of the Ten Commandments. It is part of the Torah, which is the most important book in Judaic tradition. Jesus taught that the rich should help the poor, but did not force them to do it. He did make clear what the consequences of the wrong choice would be - the forfeit of heaven. Islamic tradition emphasizes fairness and that hell is waiting for the greedy. Jesus said, "The poor will always be with you." (John 12:8) Some will always be sick, disabled, or make unwise decisions.

Rosser contends that one reason for the breakup of Yugoslavia was the resentment caused by redistribution of income from the prosperous to the poor provinces[97]. The same tension may be playing out in the European Economic Community. One can speculate that a committed voluntary effort would engender a more cooperative spirit. Remember the principle of physics that an action causes an opposite reaction. When wealth is taken by force and redistributed, the person from whom it is taken is bound to feel resentment.

Eastern religions emphasize the power of karma. Envy is a negative emotion and draws bad karma. Other negative emotions, such as anger, hate, and depression can follow. If one can replace envy with ambition, then positive karma can result. The individual can then pursue productive activities to achieve goals. In order to convince people to do this, the economic system must be fair enough to provide a chance for success.

5.7 Structure and Dynamics of Compassionate Capitalism

The system is based on free market capitalism, because it is unmatched for providing economic growth and individual freedom. Those who believe in communism or socialism should be free to join communes, establish cooperatives, or become entrepreneurs. It must be just and ethical. All companies should be encouraged, not forced, to help others overcome obstacles and succeed economically. The system must have the goal of

---

[97] Rosser, loc. cit., p. 390.

increasing income and wealth at all levels. Chapter 6 will analyze the roles of individuals and companies.

Educators should re-dedicate themselves to the development of each student to his or her maximum potential. The curriculum should not be "dumbed down," which could bore bright students. At the same time, every effort must be made to ascertain why low-performing students are having difficulty. Diagnostic tests, adjustment to accommodate learning style, or peer-to-peer learning may be necessary.

Learning is an individual experience. No one can be forced to learn or succeed. For any number of reasons, some people refuse to cooperate in their own development. Sometimes the person lacks the maturity to learn at the normal age. The door to education should be left open to allow late bloomers to obtain an education. Adult education has enabled many to establish new careers.

Government can operate as a destructive force in the economy if it interferes in markets or stifles innovation. History is replete with examples of price controls, which resulted in shortages. Excessive and complex regulations limit the freedom of innovators. The role of government will be explored further in Chapter 7.

The success or failure of Compassionate Capitalism will depend on whether each individual, company, and government agency is committed to its success. Some opposition can be expected from all directions. Lassez-faire capitalists will complain that corporations answer only to their shareholders, and have no responsibility to assist the poor. Hopefully, they can realize that helping the underprivileged is in a company's self-interest. Committed socialists will not be satisfied with any inequality in income distribution. They will need to be convinced that the system is fair. Some government officials may not wish to give up their control over others. Hopefully, these individuals will be few in number and overwhelmed by a vast majority, who can see the possibilities of shared prosperity.

An over-arching necessity is that a vast majority of individuals, companies, and government officials conduct their activities with the highest level of integrity. It may be depressing to observe how far we have drifted from this objective, but it is not impossible to recover.

PART III

TODAY AND TOMORROW

In Part II, the basic principles of Compassionate Capitalism were derived through a rational analysis of moral history, a clear understanding of the role of innovation on economic growth, and two principles of liberation theology.

Following a vast literature search, I have determined that the trail has already been blazed. In Part III individuals, as well as small, medium, and large companies have developed projects that may be described as compassionate.

Chapter 6

Roles of Individuals and Companies in a New Traditional Economy

*"What we need is not an economy of hands and heads,
but an economy of hearts."
-Gary Hamel in "Leading the Revolution"[98]-*

6.1 Introduction

Many of us can remember the old days, when our parents sealed a deal with a handshake. Some of us can recall our mothers cooking or bagging food to help a sick neighbor, or someone who had lost their job. People worked hard for companies, who in return would keep them employed through their entire careers.

Today, contracts are very complex documents which contain numerous pages, small print, and complicated legal vocabulary. In our current transient society, we don't always know our next-door

---

[98] G. Hamel, *Leading the Revolution*, Harvard Business School Press, 2000, p. 250.

neighbors, nor their problems. Employees migrate through multiple jobs in search of better opportunities. Companies engender insecurity by continually cutting jobs in order to reduce costs.

What happened? How did we lose our ethics and empathy for one another? Like most sociological phenomena, there are likely to be multiple factors involved. Traditional religious values are being challenged by the moral relativism of a secular society. New communication technologies, such as e-mail, texting, and social media, have supplanted personal contact. Entertainment technologies, which were unavailable 40 years ago, have eroded our disposable income and available time. We may be better off materially, but are we poorer morally and socially?

6.2 A Positive Role for the Individual

Implementing Compassionate Capitalism doesn't require us to roll back our technologies or basic beliefs to the 1950s. We should, however, re-commit to the behaviors that characterized the Greatest Generation.

6.2.1 Personal Integrity

Integrity may be defined as a consistency of behavior with core values. Visualize the following situation. You consider yourself to be an honest person. In a fast food restaurant, you pay for your meal with a $10 bill. The busy cashier gives you change for $20. Do you say, "Hey, you gave me too much change?" Do you rationalize by thinking that it was their mistake, and besides, the giant corporation makes billions of dollars. If you made the latter choice, there is a discrepancy between your action and your core values.

110

In our daily personal and business transactions, we should be truthful, honest, reliable, and respectful. If everyone behaved in this way, the world would be a much better place. There would also be an economic advantage. Mutual trust might lead to simpler agreements and lower transaction costs. John Huntsman, in his concise, straight-talk book, describes ten principles of individual behavior that are widely accepted[99]. Of course, not everyone will behave according to these rules. However, aside from sociopaths, personal conscience will recognize unethical behavior. In the social media age, adverse effects on reputation may be a deterrent to bad behavior. In the old days, an individual could tell a dozen or so people about a dishonest person. Multiple studies have shown that it is much harder to re-establish trust than to establish it initially.

Huntsman recounts a personal example of what it means to keep one's word[100]. In 1986, Huntsman was negotiating a deal to sell a business to Great Lakes Chemical. A price of $54 million was agreed upon and sealed with a handshake. By the time the contracts were written, the value of the business had increased to $250 million. The head of Great Lakes offered to reset the price and split the difference. Huntsman refused and insisted on the agreed price of $54 million. It was an indication of how much he valued his word – to at least $196 million.

But in reality, how do we keep a tally of who has integrity and who does not? Social media is a powerful tool, but is suffering major challenges to its own integrity. Companies can recruit friends or pay people to write favorable reviews. On the other hand, blackmailers can threaten to ruin a company's reputation,

---

[99] J. Huntsman, *Winners Never Cheat: Everyday Values We Learned as Children*, Wharton School Publishing, 2005.
[100] Ibid., pp. 81-82.

unless they are paid off. Recently, many professional photographers received e-mails threatening an avalanche of bad reviews unless the photographers paid hundreds of dollars. Competitors can anonymously malign a company through surrogates.

The internet has been described as the Wild West with no sheriff in town. What is needed is a group of referees who can throw the penalty flag on unethical practices. Consumer Reports for products and Angie's List for services are showing the way. The Better Business Bureau can be accessed online, or over the phone, to obtain information on individual businesses. For example, a potential customer can find out how many complaints have been filed, and how many have been resolved. However, the best protection is still *caveat emptor*.

Of course Federal, State, and Local governments have an obligation to use their police powers to protect their citizens from criminal activity. This will be described in more detail in Chapter 7. Hopefully, a significant number of people can be persuaded that a reputation for truthfulness and integrity is in their own best interest. Truthful people don't have the stress of trying to remember which lies they've told, or constantly look over their shoulders, wondering when they're going to be caught.

6.2.2 Helping Others

The Golden Rule tells us to treat others as we would like to be treated. It might be as simple as shoveling an elderly neighbor's sidewalk or helping a child to understand math. The first place to look is in one's own neighborhood. Of course, if you live in a wealthy suburb, you might need to look a little further, like in a poorer section of a nearby city. For busy people, it is often easier to simply write a check to a charity, and there's nothing wrong with that. However, it's a good idea to vet the charities to get the maximum benefit for a donation[101]. Every dollar spent on management and fund raising is a dollar that's not spent on the charity's mission. A good charity should spend at least 75% on its cause. Unfortunately, there are sleazy sham charities, who swindle money from unsuspecting donors. They often use sound-alike names that resemble those of well-known legitimate charities. Four cancer charities in Tennessee were accused by the Federal Trade Commission of committing massive fraud[102]. According to the FTC, the organization distributed only 3% of donations to charitable activities. The bulk of the funds went to the family running the charities in the form of high salaries, bonuses, and lavish personal expenses.

One problem with monetary donations alone is the onset of donor fatigue. Fundraising lists are often shared with, or sold to, other organizations. Eventually, the phone continuously rings and the mailbox is stuffed to overflowing. The money leaves the account every month, but you don't get to see any results.

Donating time yields immediate feedback. It is immensely satisfying to see the look of wonder on the face of a child who has just learned something new, or the satisfaction of a homeless person enjoying their first meal in several days. These experiences remind us that someone is using our donations to do something similar.

---

[101] For example, check the ratings on http://www.charitynavigator.org.
[102] R. R. Ruiz, The New York Times, March 19, 2015
http://www.nytimes.com/2015/05/20/business/4_cancer_charities_are_accused _of_fraud.

6.2.3 Mentoring

John Huntsman contends that the responsibility of a leader is to develop other leaders. This can be broadened to apply to many personal interactions. Mentoring can be a two-way street. You can learn something from everyone you meet. As a young scientist, I learned this lesson in an old food ingredient plant. The operators and supervisors all had 30+ years of experience. Together, we learned to produce a new product using ancient equipment. Listening is critical to understand the other person's goals. The first step in giving directions is to find out exactly where the person wants to go.

Sometimes mentoring roles can be dramatically reversed. A very successful investor was walking down the street when he saw an older man lying in an alley. He recognized the older man as his former mentor, who had taught him all the skills that had allowed him to become wealthy. The older man had become a crack cocaine addict and, as a result, had lost everything. The investor picked up his old mentor, cleaned him up, and persuaded him to enter a drug rehab program. The rewards of mentoring are not always that dramatic, but the satisfaction of helping someone succeed is usually sufficient.

6.3 The Roles of Companies and Organizations

In a capitalist free market economy, businesses and investors nominally drive the train. Their main goal is to make a profit. If they consistently lose money, they will eventually declare bankruptcy or be acquired. This will adversely affect employees, creditors, and investors. The simplest business organization structure is the sole proprietorship. The owner invests his own money and makes all the decisions. A partnership is formed by two or more people, who jointly own the enterprise. Initial investment, responsibilities, and profit/loss distribution are spelled out in a partnership agreement. The corporation, with its charter, bylaws, stock ownership, and Board of Directors, is the most complicated. In the 2012 U.S. presidential election, a question was raised as to whether a corporation was a person. Corporate laws define a corporation as a single entity, with many of the same rights and responsibilities as a person.

In a free enterprise economy, all individuals have the right to start a business - or band together to form a partnership or corporation. The businesses have the right to manufacture and market products, buy materials, advertise, and seek loans and investments. Some of these rights are limited by regulations designed to protect the public. For example, zoning laws restrict hazardous manufacturing to designated industrial areas. Advertising for tobacco products has been outlawed in order to protect children from becoming addicted to cigarettes.

6.3.1 A Call to Restore Business Integrity

Businesses also have responsibilities. For example, corporations must consider the needs of shareholders, customers, employees, and society. An essential principle in Compassionate Capitalism is integrity. Owners and employees of a business must be honest in all their transactions. A good benchmark from the preceding section would be John Huntsman, who lost millions of dollars by keeping his word. For those who are not as scrupulously honest as Mr. Huntsman, there are practical reasons for running an ethical business:

We are living in an age of social media. Unhappy customers can turn on their computers and tell the whole world that they were cheated. Local TV reporters live to do stories about unscrupulous businesses. Prosecutors can launch political careers by nailing unscrupulous companies to the wall. We live in a litigation-intensive society, where aggrieved consumers will sue or complain to regulators or law enforcement. Karma will eventually get you! Conversely, customers feel more comfortable doing business with a business that values integrity. Guidelines for developing practices of integrity have been proposed by Gostick and Telford[103].

Unethical business practices drive up transaction costs for everyone. Lawsuits, bankruptcies, complex contracts, and background checks can slow transactions to a snail's pace.

Government regulations are expanding at an incredible rate. Legislators and regulators build better mousetraps to deal with ever smarter mice. Honest business people unfairly bear the compliance costs.

At the end of the millennium, Enron was regarded as one of the most innovative companies in the United States[104]. The company transformed itself from an ordinary pipeline company into an energy trading company. Through long-term contracts, it shielded its customers from price fluctuations in volatile energy markets. Enron's trading practices were similar to those of hedge funds. Like some hedge funds, it encountered a series of large losses. The company pursued the dark side of innovation. They hid the liabilities off the balance sheet in offshore accounts. Meanwhile, they continued to raise cash from investors and employees. When it all collapsed, senior managers went to prison. This is an example where integrity outweighs motivation.

---

[103] A. Gostick and D. Telford, *The Integrity Advantage*, 3rd Edition, Gibbs Smith Publisher, 2003.
[104] Hamel, loc. cit., pp. 217-23.

Auto dealers, along with politicians, have been rated very low in many surveys on trust. Many consumers describe buying a car as a stressful experience. Particularly frustrating is the time-consuming process of negotiating a fair price, only to be blind-sided by additional costs for dealer prep fees, dealer-installed accessories, and expensive warranties. Earl Stewart, a West Palm Beach Toyota dealer, saw the light and publicly called out his fellow dealers on these and other unethical practices. His book, *Confessions of a Reformed Car Dealer*, would be a valuable reference for buyers[105]

6.3.2 Responsibility to the Shareholders

When investors buy stock in a company, they become owners. Management has a fiduciary duty to operate the company for the benefit of the owners. Although it is difficult to do, shareholders can band together and oust the management. Active investors can demand seats on the Board of Directors or put initiatives up for a vote at the annual meeting. Investors can also vote with their wallets and sell their shares.

Information is power. Companies have a fiduciary responsibility to provide material information to all shareholders on matters affecting the performance of the business. In the past, some managements used to provide this information to selected large investors and brokers. Asymmetric information gave these selected individuals an unfair advantage in the stock and bond markets. The Securities and Exchange Commission (SEC) now requires equal access for everyone.

---

[105] E. Stewart, *Confessions of a Reformed Car Dealer*, Middle River Press, 2012.

6.3.3 Responsibilities to Employees

Many companies claim that their most important asset is their work force. Then they launch waves of salary freezes and staff reductions. The quote from Gary Hamel at the top of this chapter deals with employee commitment. It is very difficult to engage the hearts of employees who don't see any opportunity within the company. Dissatisfied employees may vote to join a militant union. The pendulum would swing to the other extreme. Some workers may become complacent, since they don't have to worry about losing their jobs, no matter how poorly they perform. The company becomes less competitive and goes out of business. Everybody loses! This scenario has played out in workplaces all over the world.

The answer to this depressing picture is to create a culture of integrity, respect, and commitment. Employees at all levels should be encouraged to become innovators and generate new wealth for the company. A janitor could suggest a change that would make a production line run more efficiently. In return, the company should compensate employees for their contributions. Employees should also be encouraged to improve their education and skill levels. Paul Mitchel, the well-known cosmetic company, pays their employees well. In return, the employees were expected to work hard and be able to perform several different jobs. The greater flexibility allows Paul Mitchel to run with a very lean work force.

Of course, there will always be a problem of what should be done with underperforming employees. The first step should be to provide honest feedback and set up a plan for improvement. Some management theorists object to the cost in money and management time. However, these costs may be even greater for training a new employee. If the underperforming employee refuses to cooperate, then termination may be the only viable course of action. Amazon had an interesting option to deal with unhappy employees. They were offered a one-time cash payment in return for their voluntary resignation.

A controversial political issue has been the growth of income inequality. Much has been made of the ratio of income between CEOs and their entry level employees, often more than 100. The inequality inevitably gets worse during prolonged weaknesses in the economy. It might simply be a result of supply and demand, as well as value to the business. An uneducated and unskilled worker is easy to replace. A skilled, experienced turn-around CEO may be hard to find.

Solutions to income inequality are also controversial and hotly debated. Compassionate Capitalism proposes raising up workers at the bottom, without tearing down people at the top. Hard work, along with a passion to improve their education and experience are the best qualities to attain success. Employees should also develop innovation skills, since company growth depends on inventing new products and services. Of course, it helps a lot if companies offer encouragement and assistance. For example, Chick Fil-A and Starbucks offer scholarships to their employees. Like any solution, it will need the cooperation of dedicated employees and supportive companies.

Some companies are beginning to resemble cooperatives. Dan Price, CEO of Gravity Payments, raised the minimum annual salary for his 20 workers to $70,000. He also cut his own salary by $1 million. Traditional capitalists criticized the move and predicted difficulties for the small company. Plum Creek Timber and Lenovo have also been generous to their employees. Some companies have done away with titles and implemented a self-managed workforce. These measures are consistent with the Compassionate Capitalism belief in economic freedom. Companies should be free to construct the organization that they feel is best for their businesses. These companies will be valuable cases for economists and management theorists. Will a flat wage make workers happy or will it be seen as "golden handcuffs?" Will the new structures be able to compete against traditional corporations, like the cooperatives in Slovenia?

6.3.4 Responsibilities to Customers and Suppliers

In a competitive economy, a company's performance and survival may depend on how it treats its customers. If the quality of products and services are poor, customers have an incentive to find another company where they are better treated. Some companies may think they are immune to customer loss. Monopolists, for example, have no competitors. However, they may fall victim to substitution. An unhappy electric company customer may switch to natural gas for heating and cooking. Of course, there may be substantial switching costs, but sometimes, revenge is a powerful motivator.

An interesting case may be developing in the airline industry. A recent report described a rising tide of customer complaints. Consolidation has led to packed flights. Higher fares, additional fees, and poorer service have angered many fliers. But will they stop flying? Does the industry think it has a captive audience? Lower gasoline prices may entice leisure travelers to drive to their destinations. Business travelers have increasingly been using corporate and leased jets, and may even re-discover the timesaving benefits of video conferencing.

A standard cost-cutting practice for many companies has been to squeeze their suppliers. The results may look good in the income statement, but there may also be unintended consequences. If the supplier's inventory is short, he will have a tendency to sell to the highest paying customer. The supplier may seek lower cost materials and cheaper, less skilled labor. The end result may be lower quality or even unsafe products at the end of the supply chain. If squeezing the supplier results in his/her bankruptcy, there may be costly disruptions all along the supply chain.

Smart companies enlist their suppliers as full partners in the innovation process. Suppliers may have a different industry structure than their customers. For example, a supplier may be R&D intensive, while the customer is advertising intensive. A different pair of eyes with a different perspective can be very valuable. Partners should look for win-win situations, where both companies can make an economic profit.

6.3.5 Compassionate Commitment to the Community

Business organizations can play a very important role in Compassionate Capitalism by serving the communities in which they are located. Laissez-faire purists argue that corporations have no responsibility to carry out social activities. Of course, they should not be compelled to do so by government edicts. Nevertheless, perceptive companies recognize the benefits that they gain from community service.

Residents in the community represent potential employees, customers, and investors for the company.

Community service generates favorable publicity. Cynics may see PR as a less than noble motive, but as long as good work is being done, who cares.

Employees participating in community service have an opportunity to work together outside the office. For example, the Maxwell House division of Kraft Foods committed to build 100 homes with Habitat for Humanity. Volunteer employees had an opportunity to work side by side in a different environment. Individuals from widely disparate departments, working side by side, may discover an idea for improving a product or a process. Subordinates may have an opportunity to teach carpentry skills to their bosses. Workplace rivals may discover that they have something in common. Blessed are the peacemakers.

Of course, the community will benefit from these good works. More importantly, they may act as a catalyst to unleash the hopes and energies of community residents.

6.4 Summary

In summary, what has been described in this chapter is an economic and social ecosystem. The primary goals of this environment are preservation of individual and economic freedom, the highest level of individual and organizational integrity, equal opportunity for self-development, and a proactive effort to help the poor and disadvantaged. Of course, no one can expect 100% implementation of these goals. There will always be dishonest, manipulative, and even criminal people among us. What we can strive toward is to shift the numbers at the margin enough to allow law enforcement to get control of the situation. Such a shift could eventually provide momentum toward an economic and social revival.

Chapter 7

Government's Role in Compassionate Capitalism

"Government is not the answer to the problem.
Government is the problem."
-Ronald Reagan-

7.1 Introduction

Few subjects are as controversial as the role of government in a country's economy. Perhaps Ronald Reagan overstated his case, but he convinced enough people to get elected for two terms.

Of course governments have assumed many powers throughout history, but have also made many promises to protect their people from all malevolent forces. It has been a mixed record of statesmen and tyrannical despots. So, what have we learned from history? We still have an unacceptable number of repressive dictators. Many countries have capitalist free-market economies, a few practice pure communism, and others have hybrids of capitalism and socialism. Wars, revolutions, and elections have

123

transformed the economic landscapes of many countries. Over time, enlightened legislation and social pressure have tamed rapacious capitalism into a more humane system. China and a few other communist countries, have adopted free market principles. Perhaps if we can study the successes and failures of these experiments, we can draw some conclusions about the science of political economy.

7.2 Another Call for Integrity

Confucius believed that the government should coordinate all economic activity. He also taught that the best people should hold these positions, and that the country's leader should demonstrate the highest moral character. He felt that when the leader displayed a good example, the people would follow. Unfortunately, human weaknesses have caused many leaders to fall far short of this ideal.

Political corruption is a reality at all levels of government. Illinois has the distinction of having the most governors serving jail terms (four of the last eight). In an ironic demonstration of bipartisanship, both the Democratic and Republican parties were equally represented. News organizations asked, "What's wrong with Illinois[106]?" Perhaps the cynicism of Chicago has swept through the entire state. Voters were often heard saying, "Sure, we know they're corrupt, but they get the job done!" Evidently, they have accepted the explanation that graft, waste, and inefficiency are merely costs of doing business. In reality, they are opportunity

---

[106] a) E. Javers, Barbash, F., "Why Is Illinois So Corrupt?," http://www.politico.com/newss/stories/1208/16391.h5ml. b) "Illinois is in Good Company: Check Out the 10 Most Corrupt States in the US," http://www.huffingtonpost.com/madison-bondi, posted 06/17/2014.

costs that allow unemployment, poverty, and urban decay to persist[107].

Under Compassionate Capitalism, voters and candidates must reach an understanding on a new Magna Carta. True commitments to truth, transparency, and a work ethic must make government less corrupt and more efficient.

7.2.1 Responsibilities of Political Leaders

Candidates for political office must re-commit themselves to exclusively serving the interests of the public. They also must pledge absolute honesty and consistency in their positions on the issues. Specifically, they should:

Repudiate all *ad hominum* attacks. Defamation of an opponent does nothing to clarify or advocate for an issue. As Kirsten Powers has pointed out, it also silences open and honest debate[108].

Renounce the use of spin and linguistic gymnastics. Positions should be stated in clear unambiguous terms.

Scrupulously adhere to the letter and spirit of all ethics regulations and refrain from using creative efforts to avoid them.

Laws and regulations must be fair, simple, concise, and clear. Complex and vague laws result in misunderstandings, and can leave loopholes for those who commit fraud. Complexity drives

---

[107] "How Much Chicago Food Can Chicago Corruption Buy?," http://www.huffingtonpost.com/reboot-illinois, posted
[108] K. Powers, *The Silencing: How the Left is Killing Free Speech*, Regnery Publishing, 2015.

up the cost of enforcement and compliance, which is ultimately paid by consumers.

Admittedly, these are not easily practiced, particularly when your opponent is violating them at every appearance. Nonetheless, we don't accept the "everyone else is doing it" excuse from our children. If you are a candidate with integrity, don't be intimidated. Confront your opponent honestly and fearlessly. Remember, if you always tell the truth, you won't have to scramble to make up a story to cover up a distortion. If you are personally attacked, respond calmly, as you might with any other bully, and point out that *ad hominum* attacks are signs of a weak argument.

7.2.2 Responsibilities of Citizens

An old refrain tells us that the public gets the government it deserves. After all, voters seem to keep electing seriously flawed candidates. Perhaps we are all just too busy to examine the candidates and issues carefully. Pundits use the term "low information voters" as a pejorative to suggest that people are ignorant or apathetic. In a large population, there must be some that fit these descriptions. However, there might be other reasons why voters are cynical. They may believe that their vote doesn't matter because of vote fraud or because big donors are drowning out average voters. Worse yet, they may believe that all politicians are liars and thieves. As one stand-up comedian observed: "In order to understand politics, you have to look at the derivation of the word. Poli is from the Greek and means many. Tics are blood-sucking parasites." Hopefully, there are still enough voters that believe in the 5% rule.

One survey after another seems to conclude that people hate negative campaign tactics. So, why do politicians still use them?

They work! Campaign strategists have figured out that anger is a stronger motivator than reason. They will run deceptive attack ads or have a subservient political action committee do it for them. On election night they will pop the corks on very expensive champagne and celebrate the gullibility of the electorate. They will continue this pattern until we collectively say, STOP IT! The Dalai Lama taught that fear and anger are very destructive emotions. We can't afford to be caught up in them during political campaigns. It will cloud our judgment. However, given the preceding section, some attack ads might be true. When evaluating an ad, we need to act like a jury and ask critical questions. How much of the accusation is fact and how much is spin or exaggeration? Who is making the accusation and are they credible? What is the background and reputation of the accused? Finally, is the accusation reasonable?

Responsible citizens should accept their responsibilities to society:

- Study all issues and candidates carefully and unemotionally. Don't be manipulated by being uninformed. One presidential candidate said: "I love the under-educated." Hopefully, he meant that he would help them become educated, not that they could be easily deceived.

- Ask probing questions of your own candidates, as well as their opponents. Focus on the honesty and specificity of their answers.

- Cast your votes for candidates whose ideas are best for the community, not just for your own self-interest.

7.3 Responsibilities of Government in a New Traditional Economy

Governments are formed to serve and protect the people they govern. Generally a democracy or republic has a founding document which specifies the powers and limitations of the governing bodies. Since the authors cannot be omniscient over decades and centuries, the founding document usually specifies a procedure for making changes where they are necessary.

National governments are at the top of the pyramid. They are large organizations and have the advantage of scale and can address issues that are too large for smaller bureaucracies. Tasks like negotiating treaties or waging wars are tasks reserved for national governments. As with other organizations, as governments grow larger, they become bloated and inefficient, resulting in diseconomies of scale. One of the classic methods for determining compensation is span of control. Managers have an incentive to hire more people, manage larger assets, and submit bigger budgets in order to increase their compensation. Any attempts to reform large governments should make compensation independent of the span of control or provide larger bonuses for increasing productivity.

Large inefficient governments are not good at handling individuals or small groups. For example, Social Security has had numerous problems validating disability claims[109]. Many citizens with legitimate claims are denied, while others with false claims are approved. Lawyers representing these clients either get justice or enable them to commit fraud. Obviously, with 12 million people on disability, even the enormous bureaucracy is unable to handle the crushing volume of claims.

---

[109] S. Kroft, "Disability USA," 60 Minutes, Broadcast Date: Oct. 10, 2013, http://www.cbsnews/news/disability-usa.

Another example is the failure of the Veterans Administration to provide timely care for their patients[110]. Schedulers from several facilities are alleged to have falsified appointment schedules in order to receive bonuses. Robert McDonald, West Point graduate and former head of Procter and Gamble, was appointed Secretary of the VA and given the task of fixing the problem. He has pledged to discipline the individuals involved and hire additional medical professionals. However, reforming a large bureaucracy is like steering a super tanker through a narrow passage.

Government inefficiency and corruption are serious problems, but there is no legitimacy for the concept of collective guilt (remember the 5% rule). Most government employees are hard-working and dedicated to the missions of their agencies. Indeed, many of these scandals were exposed by whistle-blower employees that were unable to tolerate the corrupt behavior. With this solid base of support, there is no legitimate reason the government agencies cannot be reformed.

7.3.1 Responsibilities of Government in a Free Economy

In a free economy, anyone has the right to start a business in any legal enterprise. This freedom is absolutely necessary for innovation to flourish. Successful entrepreneurs can create an industry from a vision. Computer giants like IBM never seriously anticipated the hidden demand for home and small business computing. Steve Jobs and Bill Gates started building machines at a garage level, and grew their businesses to a global scale. Michael Dell started building customized PCs in a dorm room and pioneered a new channel of distribution. Today's entrepreneurs

---

[110] a) http://www.cbsnews.com/feature/va-hospitals-scandal, b) www.foxnews.com/politics/2014/11/10/va-secretary.

face a mountain of complex regulations at the local, regional, state, federal, and even global level. Ken Langone, the founder of Home Depot, has often stated that he would never have been able to succeed under current regulations. Uber and Aire B&B, representing the sharing economy, are in hand-to-hand combat with local governments and established businesses that are fighting for survival.

The United States Declaration of Independence states that a government derives its powers from the consent of the governed. It is natural for citizens to expect the government to protect them from harm. The question then becomes: How do governments decide what level of regulation is necessary and efficient? How do they decide what is necessary to protect one group without inadvertently damaging another group? An obvious solution is to fully inform the public, propose legislation and/or regulations, and consider feedback from an informed public. Historically, this is the process the United States has employed. Likewise, it would seem unwise to use secret panels to decide policy, and then deceive the public in order to implement the regulations. Once citizens discover they have been deceived; trust in their leaders will evaporate; the nation may become ungovernable.

It may be instructive to take a closer look at some of the motivations behind government regulations:

- Using the 5% rule, the vast majority of citizens do not need to be regulated. They will make honest choices. On the other hand, the 5% can do an enormous amount of damage, if they occupy powerful and trusted positions. Regulation falls into a vicious cycle of better mousetraps and smarter mice.

- Some individuals have domineering personalities. One way to satisfy this predilection is to aspire to a powerful government job.

- Political motives may play a role in imposing numerous regulations. Demagogues convince their followers to accept universal stereotypes. But not every successful person is dishonest and not every person on welfare or disability is scamming the system.

- Accommodation of friends, family or constituent groups may motivate a politician to support a measure that is unnecessary. Large corporations may push for rules or standards that give them a competitive advantage.

The first item argues the necessity for reasonable regulations. The last three illustrate how abuses can creep into the system. Law makers and regulators should remember that most people that must comply with the regulations are unnecessarily burdened.

In order to be efficient, and take advantage of scale economies, governments should prioritize their activities. (Remember the principal of opportunity cost.) The highest priority should be the physical protection of its citizens. Military assets must be deployed to defend against foreign attacks and terrorism, while police powers are utilized to fight crimes of violence. Secondly, police powers should be actively protecting the physical and financial assets of honest citizens. The scope of this book will be limited to the latter priority.

7.3.1.1 Public Health and Safety

Governments have an interest in maintaining a safe and healthy population. If citizens are sick or disabled, Social Security, unemployment, and worker compensation costs are borne by government agencies. In the economy, productivity is lost by workers and caregivers. Of course the cost of human misery is incalculable. Some illnesses are self-inflicted by making poor decisions. However, attempts by government to regulate behavior result in restriction of personal freedom. Since this debate is too broad to cover here, we will focus on health and product safety that arise externally.

7.3.1.2 Assuring Safe Products in the Marketplace

Government has assumed the responsibility for protecting its citizens from unsafe products in the marketplace. Although liability laws allow actions in civil courts, the U. S. Government decided to take a proactive approach by passing the Consumer Product Safety Act in 1972. The Consumer Product Safety Commission[111] is tasked with the responsibility of preventing injuries before they occur. Many of these cases involved imported products, which make access to civil courts problematic. Some recent examples are lead paint on children's toys, Chinese drywall, and melamine-tainted pet treats. Of course there is an economic trade-off to product safety regulations. The regulatory cost must be balanced against potential harm to consumers, with heavy emphasis on the latter.

Producers and consumers can do a lot to reduce the burdens on the government. Producers need to put a strong effort behind quality assurance, for both imported and domestically-produced products. Fortunately, most companies with investments in brand image already do this. Consumers must educate themselves on using the product correctly, i.e. by reading the directions. Consumers should also notify companies when they observe a problem with a

---

[111] http://www.cspc.gov.

product. Many producers provide an 800-number or a link to their websites. Problems caught early can avert recalls and damage to brand equity.

Federal and state governments began to take serious notice of worthless and unsafe medical formulations in the second half of the 19th century. Harvey Wiley, chief chemist in the Department of Agriculture, exposed unsafe adulterants in foods and medications from 1887-1902. Public outrage led to passage of the Federal Food and Drugs Act in 1906. The Bureau of Chemistry, which would evolve into the Food and Drug Administration[112], was assigned responsibility for enforcement. Cosmetic safety was added to their scope by the Federal Food Drug and Cosmetic Act[113] in 1973.

Consumers should educate themselves about the safe use of medications by reading the inserts that come with prescription drugs and raising questions with physicians and pharmacists. Supplements remain largely unregulated. The products do not have to provide the same proof of effectiveness as prescription drugs. Germany does require strong evidence of efficacy, and this should be considered when evaluating supplement claims.

7.3.1.3 Assuring Worker Safety

There are many jobs that are inherently dirty and unsafe. For example, mining, construction, and chemical processing involve a variety of hazards. The Occupational Safety and Health Administration (OSHA) is responsible for keeping workplaces as safe as possible. In order to do this, the agency may require employers to modify processes or equipment, provide protective

---

[112] http://www.fda.gov.
[113] United States Congress, *A Brief Legislative History of the Food Drug and Cosmetic Act*, University of Michigan Library, 1974.

clothing, and conduct employee training. OSHA will conduct inspections and impose fines if serious and repeated violations are found.

Workers, employers, and the government should act as a team to maintain a safe workplace. Unfortunately, the saying "familiarity breeds contempt," applies to the workplace. Employers and workers may find the safety procedures inconvenient or time-consuming. Safety equipment gets lost or is borrowed by another department. Lax attitudes creep in, setting the stage for a serious accident.

7.3.1.4 Protecting the Environment

The Environmental Protection Agency (EPA) was created to study and correct massive pollution problems in the wake of industrial development. Regulations have been enacted under the authorization of the Clean Air and Clean Water Acts. Analytical chemistry has developed methods to detect lower and lower levels, in some cases down to parts per trillion. This is a mixed blessing, since we are now forced into a debate about what is a safe level for each of these contaminants. In the interim, our moral obligation is to do the best we can with the latest information. Eventually, we can incorporate risk analysis to forecast which products are likely to be found hazardous.

One of the most acrimonious political debates concerns climate change, and whether it is caused by humans. Proponents claim that the majority of climatologists believe in both postulates. However, the scientific method is not a popularity contest. It is a slow march from hypothesis to theory to law, where scientific truth is determined by well-controlled experiments, replication, and the absence of contradictory facts and data. In the case of the climate, what is normal variability? What is the predictive value of several decades of data for a planet that has been around for millions of years? Skeptics object to a carbon tax solution, referring to it as a shakedown. Does this mean we should do nothing? In Compassionate Capitalism, innovators are encouraged and empowered to continue to develop technologies like LED lighting, low-cost recyclable batteries, and more efficient solar cells.

Every citizen has a moral obligation to conserve scarce resources and refrain from polluting the environment. Except for egregious cases, this should be a voluntary free commitment. In most cases, there is little or no monetary cost to responsible behavior, but only a little extra effort. In some situations, there is an economic benefit. For example, cutting back on utilities saves money. Some recent surveys report that American families throw away $600 of food annually. This is not only a significant loss to the household budget, but excess consumption raises food prices. If the vast majority of citizens sign on to conservation, the combination with innovation can dramatically improve our inventory of natural resources.

7.3.2 Protection of Investors

This subject usually raises the political question, "Why do greedy investors need to be protected?" Most people are investors, even if they don't realize it. If you have a savings account, an IRA, or a 401K, you are an investor. If you are a teacher or a municipal employee, your pension plan is an investor. If you are a student, you are investing your time and energy to become part of the economic system. It seems that every day we encounter stories about people who have lost their life savings to a scam artist. Compassionate Capitalism would encourage everyone to save and invest in order to become self-reliant. Successful investors do not need assistance from the government and are able to contribute to help the poor.

Government must use its police powers to protect honest saver/investors. The term "white collar crime" has a cachet that suggests that somehow it is less serious. Are we suggesting that our young people should emulate financial con artists rather than leaders of street gangs? On the federal level, a number of agencies are responsible for stopping fraud in financial rackets.

7.3.2.1 Protection of Bank Deposits

The Federal Reserve Bank was created by the Federal Reserve Act of 1913, following a series of bank failures. It is a private entity, which is overseen by the federal government. Its function is to lend money to banks to ensure their liquidity.

During the Great Depression, many banks became insolvent and simply closed their doors. Individual and commercial customers lost all their deposits. For many, financial activity devolved into the antiquated barter system. Unfortunately, those without skills or physical assets became homeless customers of the soup kitchens. The Federal Deposit Insurance Corporation (FDIC) was created in 1933 to insure bank deposits up to a limit of $2,500. Currently, the limit is $250,000 per bank per customer. The FDIC imposes regulations to ensure the financial health of banks and savings institutions.

Even with the FDIC and Federal Reserve in place, in 2008 Lehman Brothers failed, placing other financial firms in a liquidity crisis. In this crisis, the financial system froze up. No one wanted to lend money to the next company to fail. Real estate values collapsed. Homeowners and investors walked away from their properties, flooding the market with foreclosures and short sales. So who was at fault? There was plenty of blame to spread around. Banks and mortgage companies created collateralized debt obligations (CDOs) and then took on higher risk borrowers to feed the surging demand. Borrowers falsified income on their applications to qualify for mortgages. These were cynically called "liar loans," which were actually felonies. Appraisers were pressured to inflate values to justify larger mortgages. Speculators purchased multiple properties, often using liar loans, in order to make large profits through flipping. Large banks were blamed in the media and public opinion polls. They were bailed out by government loans because they were too big to fail.

Consequences of this debacle were swift and broad. The Federal Reserve arranged for weak financial institutions to be acquired by stronger firms. Ironically, banks that were too big to fail became even bigger. The fed funds rate was also dropped to near zero. This was a big blow to savers, like senior citizens, who relied on fixed income holdings for income, but it allowed banks almost free access to capital. The low rates also forced investors into riskier investments in order to obtain returns that would stay ahead of inflation. The Dodd-Frank Wall Street Reform and Consumer Protection Act placed severe restrictions on financial institutions whose failure would pose systemic risk. It also created another government agency to protect consumers.

The financial disaster of 2008 illustrates an unfortunate flaw in our culture. Although there may only be a minority of banks, mortgage companies, and speculators that are corrupt, they can persuade normally honest people to do dishonest things.

Compassionate Capitalism must emphasize personal responsibility. We must be alert to a defect in our character that goes all the way back to the Garden of Eden, where Adam blamed Eve for his sin, and Eve in turn blamed the serpent. Sometimes we have to look in the mirror and ask ourselves, "Did I have any responsibility for this, and if so, how can I help fix it?"

Gerard L. Hasenhuettl

7.3.2.2 Protecting Investments

Owning shares of a business has a long history. Commenda contracts were commonly used in the Roman Empire. The first stock exchanges emerged during the Renaissance, allowing investors to own shares of trading companies. In New York, stocks were bought and sold under a large Buttonwood tree on Wall Street. In 1792, the Buttonwood Agreement was signed by 24 brokers to form the New York Stock and Exchange Board, which evolved into the New York Stock Exchange. The Board drew up a set of trading rules designed to prevent fraud and market manipulation.

Stock trading was a volatile experience in the nineteenth and twentieth centuries, with cycles of prosperity and panic. In the Roaring Twenties, stock prices soared and many new fortunes were made. It all came to an end with the crash of 1929 and the Great Depression. In 1934, the Securities and Exchange Commission was formed to protect investors, set accounting standards, facilitate capital formation, and ensure orderly markets. For the most part, the SEC has been successful. One glaring exception was the failure to respond to warnings about Bernard Madoff's enormous Ponzi scheme. Harry Markopoulos has written a fascinating account of mathematical evidence that was repeatedly ignored by the SEC[114].

Although government regulation is robust, in too many cases it is reactive. Individual investors must do their part by being educated and informed. Once your money is missing from an insured account, it is almost impossible to get it all back. The educational system has begun to recognize the importance of financial literacy. Students need to know how to budget, save, and invest.

---

[114] H. Markopoulos, *No One Would Listen: A True Financial Thriller*, Wiley, 2011.

At the other end of the age spectrum, the elderly need to be educated on how to spot a scam. One contact list identified potential customers as "gullible old people."

Con artists devise schemes to appeal to our deep-seated greed and other repressed human weaknesses. If someone asks you to invest in something illegal, hang up the phone or shred the letter. If the person doesn't pay you, would you go to the police and admit you were conspiring to break the law? Investors should consider the axiom, "if something looks too good to be true, it probably is."

7.3.3 Protecting Intellectual Property[115]

As noted previously, innovation and technology are critical for economic growth. The reward for creative individuals is recognition by government that the innovator has the exclusive right to sell and distribute their product or service. Failure to provide this protection would likely deter the innovator from making the effort, particularly if a substantial investment of time or capital is involved.

An inventor can apply for a product or process that is novel and non-obvious. The United States was initially a first-to-invent country, but a few years ago, changed to a first-to-file system[116]. Obtaining a patent is often a difficult adversarial process, with a government examiner playing devil's advocate. Competitors or others can initiate interference procedures. Sometimes outsiders may file actions as a blackmail scheme. Hiring a patent attorney can be an expensive, but often necessary, investment.

---

[115] A. Poltorak, I., Lemel, P. J, *Essentials of Intellectual Property: Law, Economics, and Strategy*, Second Edition, Wiley, 2011.
[116] M. H. Heines, *First to file Patents for Today's Scientist and Engineer*, Wiley-AICHE, 2014.

Copyrights[117] and trademarks[118]are necessary to protect the creative work of writers, artists, and businesses. Again, the time and expense should be minimal, compared to the protected creative work.

Enforcement of intellectual property protection is carried out in the courts, using the government document as evidence. This can be as simple as a "cease and desist" letter, or as complex as extended litigation. International protection is governed by treaties; this may be difficult, since cooperation of another country is needed. Communist countries, for example, are not enthusiastic about the concept of private property.

7.4 The Supportive Role of Government

Prior to the Great Depression, the United States was a country, which practiced rugged individualism. When people got sick or lost their jobs, they were cared for by their extended family and friends. When the resources were inadequate, private charities often took up the burden. Financial panics and rough patches were known, but the Depression was deep and long-lasting. The subsequent election of Franklin D. Roosevelt represented a turning point in the social contract between the U. S. Government and its people. Policies were enacted to create a safety net for people in trouble. Some programs, like the Works Progress Administration (WPA), did not survive. The following discussion will focus on some that have endured.

---

[117] M. LaFrance, *Copyright Law in a nutshell,* Second Edition, west Academic Publishing, 2015.
[118] M. LaFrance, *Understanding Trademark Law*, Second Edition, Lexisis/Nexis, 2009.

7.4.1 Social Security[119]

In 1935, President Roosevelt signed the Social Security Act[120]. The first taxes were collected in 1937, and the first monthly benefits began to be distributed in 1940. The principle goal of the law was to force individuals to save toward their retirement. In the years that followed, other programs were added: Disability, Medicare, and Supplemental Security Income (SSI).

In order to finance this massive program, the Social Security Trust Fund was established. Inputs to the Fund were payroll taxes, divided equally between workers and their employers. Initially, the ratio of workers to retirees was high. As the years passed, this ratio declined, most likely due to increases in life expectancy, millions of abortions, and a large increase in self-employed. However, the biggest problem was that the Fund was a large piggy bank that was too much of a temptation for politicians to resist. Congress began to borrow money to fund pet projects. The Fund is left holding government bonds. Currently, the debt owed to the Fund is $2.5 trillion. With the Treasury bonds yielding such low rates, the Fund is in danger of losing money to inflation.

Social Security recipients constitute a diverse population. Some are wealthy and could easily manage without benefits. Some in the middle haven't quite saved enough to live comfortably without benefits. Many more depend solely on Social Security to survive. Reasons for this situation are myriad and complex, so no stereotype can provide an explanation. Compassionate Capitalism urges those who are better off to help the elderly poor in their communities. Private local efforts can decrease the load on less efficient federal programs.

---

[119] http://www.ssa.gov.
[120] D. Beland, *Social Security: History and Politics from the New Deal to the Privatization Debate*, University Press of Kansas, 2005.

7.4.2 Unemployment Insurance

For a worker, living from one pay period to another, loss of a job due to layoff or injury can be devastating. When wages stop, bills are not paid, utilities are cut off, cars are repossessed, and families are evicted. The resources of family, friends, and neighbors are depleted as they rally to assist the afflicted worker. If unemployment is widespread, businesses offering discretionary goods and services lose income. Music stores, restaurants, and jewelers may close, causing still more unemployment.

In 1932, the State of Wisconsin enacted the first unemployment insurance program. Three years later, the program served as a template for the Social Security Act[121]. Unemployment insurance is a cooperative State and Federal effort. The Federal Government sets the standards, so no state will have an advantage over others. The Treasury Department set up a fund, with a separate account for each state. The states administer the program: setting eligibility requirements, collecting premiums from employers, keeping records, and paying claims from their accounts.

7.4.3 Worker's Compensation

The idea of compensating workers for injuries dates back to ancient Sumaria[122]. In the feudal systems of the Dark Ages, the

---

[121] a) K. Downey, *The Woman Behind the New Deal: the Life and Legacy of Frances Perkins, Social Security, Unemployment Insurance*, Anchor, Reprint Edition, 2010., b) D. F. Schloss, *Insurance Against Unemployment*, Leopold Classic Library, 2015.

[122] G. Guyton, "A Brief History of Workers Compensation," Iowa Orthopedic Journal 19-106-110 (1988).

individual nobleman was morally obligated (*noblesse oblige*) to take care of their serfs.

The early history of industrialization was characterized by experimentation with methods of production. Entrepreneurs often didn't fully understand the underlying physical and chemical principle of their processes. Machine techniques were imprecise and not standardized. Accidents became more frequent. Steam engines exploded, limbs were amputated by cutting tools, and toxic chemicals were released into enclosed spaces. Workers who were not killed were often incapacitated. Some employers were compassionate and helped the families. Others regarded the tragedies as accidents, or even blamed the employees of causing the accidents by their negligence. Employees could sue the employers in Europe, Britain, and the United States, but they were frequently unsuccessful. In 1894, Otto von Bismarck implemented a workers compensation and medical care system in Prussia. It expropriated a demand from Marxist opponents.

In the United States, a reform movement began in the early twentieth century, partly driven by Upton Sinclair's 1906 novel "The Jungle." He described the plight of an immigrant disabled in a Chicago meat packing plant. Starting with Wisconsin in 1911, almost all states passed uniform workers compensation laws. This was a grand compromise. Companies paid for the insurance, but received immunity from lawsuits. Workers received prompt compensation for their injuries. The federal government added Social Security disability in the 1930s. This federal-state partnership has lasted for over 75 years.

7.4.4 Public Assistance

Prior to the twentieth century, families, friends, neighbors, and charities took care of the poor. Increased production sometimes caused employee errors. During times of economic distress, these resources were stretched beyond their limits. States began to take notice, and by 1926, 40 states had established public relief services. The state programs were described as relief for the "worthy poor," which we described earlier as the "involuntary poor."

The Great Depression quickly overwhelmed the resources of the state plan. In 1932, President Hoover signed the Emergency Relief and Constriction Act. This legislation established a $300 million fund to assist distressed states. In 1935, President Roosevelt signed the Federal Emergency Relief Act, which covered many more people. Social Security meshed with welfare to support children, the elderly, and the disabled. Medicare and the WIC program were added later. After World War II, welfare became a multi-generational phenomenon. Teenagers were urged by their families and friends to "sign up for a check." In 1996, President Clinton and Speaker Newt Gingrich worked together to pass the Personal Responsibility and Work Opportunity Reconciliation Act. It reformed the Aid to Families with Dependent Children (AFDC) system, requiring able-bodied adults to actively seek employment while receiving benefits. At about the same time, Britain and France enacted similar reforms to deal with their surging public relief expenditures. To soften the impact, education, childcare, and housing assistance programs were enacted at state and federal levels.

7.4.5 Housing Assistance

Government involvement began in the nineteenth century, in an effort to provide shelter for those who could not afford to buy or rent. As in other assistance programs, federal, state, and local agencies are involved in a complicated network. The federal government sets the rules and provides funding. Local agencies administer the actual assistance. In the mid-twentieth century, large housing complexes, colloquially known as "the projects," were built. Some were converted military barracks, some were hastily built with shoddy materials, and some were solidly built. Some urban complexes became havens for gangs and drug dealers. Honest tenants were terrorized and repair contractors were afraid to show up and fix things. Buildings began to deteriorate.

Academics and politicians began to debate the effects of concentrating poverty in small geographic areas. The Federal Affordable Housing Act of 1990 began a new trend. Section 8 rent subsidies were issued to residents of public housing, allowing them to rent from private landlords. Massive complexes, like Cabrini Green and the Robert Taylor Homes in Chicago[123], were demolished and redeveloped. As in many social changes, one set of problems was exchanged for another. In Cook County, there is a formidable waiting list for Section 8 vouchers. Close-in Chicago suburbs have mandated landlord workshops to deal with increasing gang and drug activity. On the positive side, tenants have been freed from the stigma of "the projects." Many are taking advantage of education assistance to build better self-sufficient lives for themselves and their children.

7.4.6 Medicaid Care

Doctors have traditionally chosen their careers because they are compassionate people. They often cared for indigent patients and waived their fees. There was very little cost involved for treating a few extra patients. Catholic hospitals and nursing homes took care of indigent patients at reduced or no fee. Local governments

---

[123] D. B. Hunt, *Blueprint for Disaster: The Unraveling of Chicago Public Housing*, University of Chicago Press, Reprint Edition, 2010.

operated nursing homes for the indigent, which varied in their quality of care. Many were motivated to work hard because they did not want to end up in the "poor house."

In the second half of the twentieth century, the situation changed rapidly. The costs of medical education, malpractice insurance and medical equipment skyrocketed. Governments and insurance companies insisted on a mountain of paperwork. Doctors were pressured to see as many paying patients as possible, just to meet expenses. In 1965, the Social Security Administration added Title XIX to the Code of Federal Regulations, establishing Medicaid[124]. States established eligibility criteria and administered the program, while the federal government paid a large portion of the cost. Currently, Medicaid is the largest insurer in the United States.

In 2009, the Patient Protection and Affordable Care Act (PPACA) passed the U. S. Congress on a straight party-line vote[125]. Rather than target uninsured, the ACA sought to overhaul the entire medical care system. The measure required all citizens to purchase health insurance, or pay a fine. It offered subsidies to those who could not afford the insurance premiums. The ACA also required the states to expand Medicaid to everyone earning less than 133% of the poverty level. The program got off to a rocky start. The healthcare.gov website crashed and sign-up deadlines had to be extended. Many people lost their doctors and insurance. Large primary care networks replaced M.D.s with physician-assistants and nurse-practitioners. At the end of 2015, about 30 million remain uninsured. A definitive report card for the ACA will come with statistics on mortality and morbidity.

---

[124] A. B. Cohen, *Medicare and Medicaid at 50: America's Entitlement Programs in the Age of Affordable Care*, Oxford University Press, 2015.
[125] E. D. Kinney, *The Affordable Care Act and Medicare in Comparative Context*, Cambridge University Press, 2015.

7.5 Looking to the Future

The concept of Compassionate Capitalism posits that integrity is essential for individuals, businesses, and government, in order for this new traditional economy to succeed. The national debt of the United States is approaching $20 trillion. Large quantities of dollars, whether for Hurricane Katrina relief or a gas station in Afghanistan, have become invisible to the accounting system. No one can answer the simple question, "Where was the money spent?" Recovery from the Great Recession of 2008 is the weakest since World War II. If these trends continue, service on the debt may threaten essential programs.

The social safety net was built several strands at a time. Each program is a complex partnership with the states, local governments, and contractors. Each program tends to branch out and provide more services. At the current time, do we have a safety net or a giant Gordian knot? It seems reasonable that there could be a lot of duplication and holes in the net.

Given the above situation, we need an impeccably honest and highly effective government, if elections are honest, we are the government. We must elect honest and skilled candidates to run our government machinery. Unfortunately, the current polarized two-party system only serves up selective outrage. Partisans can only see evil in the opposing party. Perhaps we need to establish an Honest Majority Party.

Once we have principled leaders, we need to insist that every dollar of fraud and wasteful spending (the opportunity cost) is reallocated. At the same time, we need to help. "See something, say something" is a motto that should be used to detect waste and fraud. In one Florida county, the local Tea Party sends a representative to every city council and county commission meeting. The representative reports on every measure that is a no-bid contract or wasteful spending. The second thing to do is help the government assist the poor. Every person lifted out of poverty can reach back to help someone else.

Chapter 8

The Faith Community and Compassionate Capitalism

"...Inasmuch as ye have done it unto one of the least of these
my brethren, ye have done it unto me."
-*Matt. 25:40*-

8.1 Introduction

The elements of Compassionate Capitalism, which we described
in Chapter 5, included prioritizing the poor and individual
development. People of faith have been carrying out these
activities since the early dawn of religious belief. They have
defined our legal systems of law and ethics and have refined their
skills to alleviate suffering. In addition to houses of worship,
people of faith built schools and hospitals. They labored to feed
the hungry and shelter the homeless. Compassionate business
organizations can learn from, support, and imitate these noble
people. Better yet, creative business people could help charities
deliver their services more efficiently.

8.2 Zooming In: Microcosm – Erie Pennsylvania

The City of Erie is a typical example of Midwestern industrial cities. Polish, Italian, German, Irish, and Russian immigrants settled into their own ethnic neighborhoods. It had sheltered ports on Lake Erie, was on a main railway line, and two U. S. highways. It was a natural place for industries to settle. Granted, lake effect snow was an obstacle to efficient transportation, but snow removal crews dealt with it efficiently. Catholic and public schools produced an educated and motivated work force. All these factors attracted diverse industries to Erie (see Table 8.1). In the post-World War I and II periods, manufacturing produced the items to rebuild war-torn Europe and Japan. The outbreak of the Korean and Cold War's further stimulated production.

Table 8.1 Erie PA Industries

American Sterilizer	Medical Equipment	Purchased by Steris Corp.; Moved out of the city.
Bucyrus Erie	Mining Equipment	Closed Erie Operations.
Erie Brewing Co.	Beer Production	Closed original plant.
Continental Rubber	Rubber Production	Closed Erie operations.
Erie Lithographing & Printing	Lithography	Moved to another city.
Erie Forge & Steel	Specialty Steel	Purchased by employees & still operates in Erie.

Erie Resistor	Electronic Components	Bought & sold by several companies.
Erie Magnetics	Magnetic Products	Changed name to Eriez Manufacturing Co.
General Electric	Appliances, Locomotives	Moved appliance operations; changed to GE Transportation.
Hammermill Paper	Paper Manufacturing	Acquired by International Paper; closed Erie plant.
Hughson Chemical /Lord Corp.	Adhesives	Moved to other cities in the area.
Mallinckrodt Chemical	Catalysts	Acquired by BASF; still operates in Erie.
Ruberoid/GAF Corp.	Roofing Materials	Closed Erie manufacturing facility.
Zurn Industries	Boilers, Heat Exchangers	Manufacturing is moving to Milwaukee.

Information kindly contributed by John Krahe; Erie Manufacturer and Business Association.

Social clubs played an important role in the development of the city[126]. Ethnic clubs were an oasis for new immigrants. They

---

[126] Information was drawn from the following resources: a) http://oldtimeerie.blogspot.com/2013/02/top-35-defunct-erie-pa-clubs; b) http://oldtimeerie.blogspot.com/2014/04/ethnic-clubs-of-erie-in-1952; c)

Gerard L. Hasenhuettl

offered English language instruction, mutual benefit insurance, and assistance in job placement. Veterans' clubs were refuges for young men returning from war. They could discuss experiences that they would not share with their families. Labor clubs were places where workers could socialize with their peers and exchange information. Wealthy Erieites had their own elegant clubs, where business deals could be discussed over a steak dinner or on the golf course. Some clubs were originally founded as singing societies. Catholic parishes also opened clubs and offered Bingo games, which attracted players from the entire tri-state area. Table 8.2 shows examples of some of these organizations. After Prohibition was repealed, clubs were allowed to serve alcohol on Sundays. With all the bars and clubs in Erie, there was no excuse for driving while intoxicated, since there was always a bar within walking distance. The 1950s and 60s were boom years for musicians. The demise of many clubs was caused by a crackdown on slot machines, loosening of the Pennsylvania blue laws, and the widespread diffusion of televisions into homes.

---

http://www.ssjm.org/ministries/hli/history-off-the-nuova-aurora-club; d) Discussions with long-time Erie residents.

152

Table 8.2 Clubs in Erie Pennsylvania

Italian	Nuova Aurora, Calabrese Club of Monte Carmelo, Caesare Batisti, Sons of Italy
Polish	Polish National Club, Polish National Alliance, Monuszko Club, Polish Sharpshooters, Polish Falcons
Russian	Russian American, CYS Club, CGS Club
Other Ethnic Clubs	Siebenburger Club, Erie Saengerbund, Danish Club, Lithuanian Club, Greek Catholic, Slovak Club, Romanian Club
Labor Club	Allied Trades Club
Social Clubs	Eagles Club, Elks Club, Moose Club, East Erie Turners
Parish Clubs	Saint Mary's, Holy Trinity, Saint Francis Ushers
Upscale Clubs	Aviation Club, Erie Club, Erie Yacht Club, Kahkwa Club, Lake Shore Country Club
Veterans Clubs	Veterans of Foreign Wars, American Legion

In the late 1950s and 1960s, the economy fell back into the normal business cycle. Layoffs occurred during periods of reduced demand. Friction began to break out between companies and unions representing their workers. Some companies, under pressure to cut costs and remain profitable, began to close down or relocate some of their operations. Today, there are only a few manufacturing firms remaining. Housing and infrastructure in the inner city have deteriorated badly. Unemployment, poverty, and reliance on government programs have risen dramatically. Erie was once the safest city in Pennsylvania, but an influx of gangs and drugs has increased violent crimes. Almost all the Catholic elementary schools have closed, leaving the public school system with a complex problem.

8.3 Heroes of Faith Rise to the Challenge

It's inevitable that in every disaster, heroes show up to save lives. In Erie, communities of faith stepped into the economic disaster and did what their faith demanded. They fed the hungry, gave shelter to the homeless, gave job skills to the uneducated, and distributed clean clothing. Let us review some of the individuals and institutions that have helped to make Erie's inner-city a better place to live.

8.3.1 Monsignor James Peterson

Father Peterson was a professor of English and theology at Gannon University, a private Catholic school located in the center of Erie. He was the antithesis of the stereotypical college professor, humble and calm. However, he could formulate logical and powerful arguments that even the best students could not counter.

Father Pete was also a great counselor. Troubled students lined up to talk to him about their problems. He would pray with, encourage, and assure them that he would always be there to help. In his spare time, he would walk across the street and visit the prisoners in the Erie County Jail.

One would think that all these activities would be enough for one person, but not Father Pete. He recognized that crime and substance abuse were tightly linked, and the Maria House Project was born.[127] The house, located in downtown Erie, accommodates 30-35 men who are recovering from addiction, incarceration, homelessness, and mental illness. It is a community of prayer,

---

[127] http://www.mariahouseproject.org.

sharing, and helping one another. Over one hundred volunteers work to support the project. As one resident said, "The moment he took my hand and said, 'let's pray,' I knew my life was going to change. Father Pete changed my life."

Monsignor Peterson passed away in 2013, but lives in the hearts of the people who knew him and in the lives of those he helped. True to his life story[128], he found Christ in the margins.

8.3.2 Emmaus Ministries

The Benedictine Order established St. Mary's Church and an elementary school on East Tenth Street, in the heart of the German-American neighborhood. Brothers of the Benedictine order were the first teachers at the school, later replaced by the Benedictine Sisters. Eventually, they added St. Benedict High School for girls and an auditorium for parish activities. For decades the schools enjoyed full enrollment, and numerous graduates went on to higher education and distinguished careers.

As industries and jobs left Erie, the neighborhood became poorer and less Catholic. The schools became more diverse, with fewer students paying full tuition. St. Mary's Church experienced lower attendance and collection revenues. Although the Benedictine Sisters tried valiantly to carry on, the Diocese closed St. Mary's, St. Benedict's, and almost all Catholic elementary schools in Erie.

The Sisters re-tasked and formed Emmaus Ministries[129], dedicated to helping the poor in the ravaged inner city neighborhood. The Sisters dove in on many fronts and attracted volunteers to help. Sister Gus's Kitchen fed the homeless and families who didn't

---

[128] J. Peterson, *More I Could Not Ask: Finding Christ in the Margins*, Crossroad Publishing Co., 1999.
[129] http://www.emmauserie.org.

have enough to afford both shelter and food. One winter night, a volunteer saw a man with plastic bags wrapped around his bare feet. The volunteer gave the man his shoes and walked home through the snow in his socks.

Just because elementary and high schools were closed did not mean that education had died on their block. The Benedictine Sisters refocused their efforts to teach job skills to unemployed adults. But their efforts did not end there. They established a day-care center to support low-income working parents. The children also benefit from being in a learning environment.

8.3.3 Gannon University

The University, where Father Peterson taught, is located in the center of downtown Erie. It was founded by Archbishop John Mark Gannon to provide higher education for the children of working class people. Tuitions were low and the students could live at home. The College offered a liberal arts core curriculum, as well as majors in sciences, engineering, and business. The Gannon community has always been a voice for morality and social conscience.

In the last 15 years, Gannon University has dramatically expanded its campus into the neighborhood; as it expanded it integrated new degree programs into its curriculum. Under the leadership of President Keith Taylor, the University committed itself to improving the surrounding neighborhood.

The West Bayfront neighborhood is bounded by West 12th Street on the south, Sassafras Street on the east, the Bayfront Highway on the west, and the Erie Bay on the north. It has approximately 15,000 residents. The University is developing a strategy for improving cohesion, safety improvements, economic opportunity, and better housing. City, county, and regional planners have been included to make their efforts synergistic. Gannon University has established Neighborhood Student Endowed Scholarships which serves students from the West Bayfront Neighborhood.

Gannon Students are involved in several programs to revitalize the neighborhood.

GO College at Strong Vincent and East High Schools (Mentoring students to increase college admission.)

Martin Luther King After-School Program (Tutoring students to improve academic achievement.)

Club Fit at Strong Vincent and East High Schools (Utilizing fitness and well-being to increase self-esteem, pride, and academic achievement.)

8.3.4 The Sisters of Mercy[130]

In 1827, Catherine McAuley, a Catholic laywoman, established a shelter in Dublin, Ireland to serve as a place of education for women and girls. In 1831, McAuley and two companions founded the Sisters of Mercy. Impressed by their good works, the Bishop of Pittsburgh, Pennsylvania invited the Sisters to come to the United States. Their ministry expanded to include education, healthcare, and social services work in hundreds of locations.

In Erie, The Order established Mercyhurst College and the House of Mercy on the east side. When the Sisters of Mercy sold their motherhouse, they used the proceeds to establish the McAuley Institute, named for their founder.

---

[130] http://www.sistersofmercy.org.

Denise is a 50-year old native of Pittsburgh. After struggling with drug addiction and the loss of her two sons, she moved to Erie and entered a rehabilitation program. Upon completion, she lived in the Mercy Center for Women. Now she is working full-time in healthcare and has her own apartment.

Now a university, Mercyhurst and the McAuley Institute teamed up with local residents to revitalize Erie's East Bayfront neighborhood, one of the oldest in the city. The area is bounded by the Bay on the north, East 6th Street on the South, Holland Street on the west, and Wayne Street on the east. Their goals included crime reduction, improvement of residential housing stock, and improvements in common areas, such as gardens, parks, and playgrounds.

8.3.5 The Sisters of Saint Joseph[131]

The Sisters of Saint Joseph in northwestern Pennsylvania had two missions. They founded Saint Vincent Hospital in Erie and Spencer Hospital in Meadville to take care of the sick and the poor. They were also largely dedicated to teaching in Erie's Catholic schools. As those schools began to close, the Sisters found another way to serve. In 2000, they launched the Neighborhood Network. The neighborhood is bounded on the north by West 12th Street, the south by West 26th Street, State Street on the east and Cranberry Street on the west. The historic Little Italy section falls within the Network.

The Sisters commissioned a study to collect demographic data for the neighborhood. They then began one-on-one advocacy for residents. A soup kitchen and food pantry feeds the hungry. Children are tutored in reading, computers, life and work skills.

---

[131] http://www.ssjnn.

Food, clothing, shelter, comfort, and spiritual guidance are lovingly provided. Many college and graduate students visited their thrift stores and decorated their apartments in "early Salvation Army." A Time Out for Moms program offers a weekly luncheon so that neighborhood mothers can get together and network.

The Genesis Home Project offers affordable rentals for families interested in future home ownership. Project volunteers work with the tenants to develop budgeting, credit repair, and home ownership skills. The goals of the program are economic opportunity and neighborhood revitalization.

The ministry has now expanded their services to the hard-hit east side, which is housed in the former St. John's School.

It might seem to the reader that the foregoing stories are obsessively Catholic. The reason is simple. Erie has been a heavily Catholic city. At its zenith, the Diocese had two dozen elementary schools, four high schools, and three colleges. Of course, many other religious and secular organizations are helping the poor and are equally commended. The other reason is geographic. If you look at a map of the inner city, the Catholic organizations have blanketed most of the area.

8.3.6 Holy Family School

Holy Family Parish was established in 1908 to meet a need for a Catholic church to minister to the Slovak community[132]. In 1915, classes were held in the basement of the small church. The parish

---

[132] History of Holy Family was kindly provided by Sister Kevin Berdis OSF

grew, and in 1949, Holy Family School opened and began to educate the children.

Catholic schools in Erie, like many other cities, were devastated by the declines in enrollment and religious order teachers. As industrial companies exited the city, job losses translated into a loss of per-capita income. Years later, the Archdiocese closed elementary schools. Holy Family on Erie's East Side, and Cathedral Elementary in the center of the city were the sole survivors.

Sister Kevin Berdis, the principal of Holy Family and the sister of professional boxer Jimmy Berdis, was determined to keep the school open. She rallied parishioners, former students, and local workers to contribute to pay tuition for neighborhood students, who could not normally afford a Catholic education. The school is hanging by a thread, but the leadership is strong and people in the neighborhood are dedicated.

8.4 Zooming Out: Working Nationally

Almost all faiths have ministries that serve the poor. As mentioned in Chapter 2, it is a central teaching of Judaic, Christian, and Islamic tradition. Sharing with the poor is intrinsic to Eastern religions that believe in karma, universal consciousness, and reincarnation. There is a strong history in the United States of charitable support worldwide through missionaries.

8.4.1 The Salvation Army

In 1865, William Booth, a London minister, noticed that destitute homeless people did not feel comfortable coming to his church.

Other parishioners were scandalized by their shabby clothes and shortcomings in personal hygiene. Booth resolved to establish a church for these people. The East London Mission opened; in 1878, it became the Salvation Army[133].

The Army caught the imagination of dedicated Christians and diffused throughout the world. Today it ministers to the outcasts, addicts, alcoholics, the homeless, and victims of disasters.

In addition to the thrift stores, the ministry raises money through private donations and those iconic red kettles. During the Christmas season, a few anonymous donors have dropped occasional gold or silver coins in those kettles.

8.4.2 Samaritan's Purse

Bob Pierce was deeply moved after visiting suffering children on the Korean island of Kojito and wrote these now famous words: "Let my heart be broken with the things that break the heart of God." In 1970, he took action and founded Samaritan's Purse to support heroic missionaries who were living among the poorest people on the planet[134].

In 1973, Pierce met Franklin Graham, son of evangelist Billy Graham. When Bob Pierce died in 1978, Franklin Graham became the President and Chairman of the Board of Samaritan's Purse. In over thirty years of following earthquakes, hurricanes, war, and famine, the ministry followed the biblical example of the Good Samaritan. Whether it's an epidemic in West Africa or a devastating flood in St. Louis, Samaritan's Purse can put volunteers on the ground and provide a wide variety of services.

---

[133] http://www.salvationarmy/ihq/history.
[134] http://www.samaritanspurse.org/ourministry/history.

8.4.3 Prison Fellowship Ministry

Charles Colson was flying high in the 1970s. As a top aide to President Nixon, he was focused on destroying political enemies before the 1972 election. When it all fell apart, he converted to Christianity and pleaded guilty to obstruction of justice in connection with the Daniel Ellsberg case. He served seven months in Alabama's Maxwell Prison.

In 1976, Colson founded Prison Fellowship Ministry. The organization, in cooperation with local churches, preached the good news of the Gospel and encouraged the prisoners to change their lives. Shocked by the abysmal conditions in prisons, Colson also became an advocate for prison reform. The organization grew to 50,000 volunteers in 88 countries.

Prison Fellowship ministers to families, as well as the prisoners. Partnering with local churches and the Salvation Army, the ministry gathers toys at Christmas time and delivers them to the children, along with a note from the imprisoned parent. During the summer, prisoners' children are taken to summer camp. This experience gives them the opportunity to play with other children and get a different perspective on life.

8.4.4 World Vision

World Vision started with one man helping one child in one country with just five dollars. It began in the 1950s with volunteers working to help orphans from the Korean War. In over 60 years, World Vision has expanded to affect over four million children in 100 countries[135].

---

[135] a) http://www.worldvision.org/about-us/our-history, b)
http://www.worldvision.org/our-impact/clean-watteerr.

World Vision has several impact areas, with projects on health services, child protection, and water treatment. The organization has the ambitious goal of bringing clean water to one child every ten seconds. The long-term goal is to provide water to every child where World Vision has operated by 2030.

Another source of pride is the organization's careful use of donor funds. Charity Navigator reports that 84.4% of revenues went to programs and 4.9% to administration. Only 0.04% is allocated to leadership compensation. Their accountability/transparency rating is 96%[136].

The technical staff works interactively with the community to educate operators to run and maintain the equipment. This collaboration has led to a very low incidence of equipment breakdown. World Vision is therefore able to move on to the next community. With so many desperately poor children in the world, the World Vision teams need to keep moving.

8.4.5 Habitat for Humanity

Millard and Linda Fuller decided to give away their fortune to help the poor. In 1976, they founded Habitat for Humanity and started building homes, even though they had little experience in this field.

The Habitat system is reminiscent of the rural barn-raising method. You helped your neighbor build a barn and the neighbor would help you to build yours[137]. Habitat also assists low-income families to finance their new or rehabilitated homes, by offering

---

[136] http://www.charitynavigator.org.
[137] http://www.habitat.org/about.

low-interest loans. The organization has over 1,400 local affiliates in the United States and 70 worldwide. Habitat has helped over 8.8 million people improve their living conditions since 1976.

Habitat raises funds from private and corporate donations, sales of donated building supplies, and mortgage repayments. Volunteers donate their time to work under the supervision of construction professionals, who are also volunteers. One notable volunteer was former President Jimmy Carter.

In the spring of 2005, the Fullers left Habitat and started the Fuller Center for Housing. The Center partners with communities worldwide to build low-cost housing for working families.

8.5 What Have We Learned?

Many of our parents and grandparents have learned the viciousness of the business cycle and the destructiveness of technical shifts. They dealt with it by helping their neighbors. The Great Depression was a time of bartering, since no one had any money. Charity began at home and spread through neighborhoods. In the current era, families and friends have been spread over the country, or even over the globe. Now it's often a case of strangers helping strangers.

Clean food and water are necessities for sustaining life. Shelter is necessary for protection from the elements. The value of quality education and job training is too often overlooked as survival skills. If one has multiple skills, it is much easier to adapt to changing technology and economic conditions. Even in a depression, it is useful to have skills that can be bartered for goods and services.

This chapter has attempted to show that if some of us are having problems, help with survival is available. People who provide care and love can inspire an optimistic attitude that is helpful in overcoming life's problems.

PART IV

WHAT IS HAPPENING NOW

In Part III we described the activities of individuals, companies, governments and people of faith. Some suggestions were made to align these activities more closely with the principles of integrity and compassion.

Part IV will discuss the implementation of this new traditional economy. Chapter 9 will show the incredible success that can spring up from the dedication of just one person. Chapter 10 will show the amplifying power of companies and their employees. Time and space will not allow a complete inventory of these activities. Rather, the following chapters will discuss selected illustrative examples. Chapter 11 will suggest strategies for companies who would like to implement a Compassionate Capitalism program in their community. Chapter 12 will challenge the financial community to assist in the formation of new businesses. These new businesses can also help to revitalize communities.

Chapter 9

The Power of One

"It is better to light a single candle than to curse the darkness."
-Ancient Chinese proverb-

9.1 Introduction to Hope

In mathematics, anything raised to the power of one remains unchanged. In the sociological realm, the power of one dedicated individual can initiate massive change. It may begin with one simple act of kindness, and either rapidly or slowly, grows into a movement. Others may notice the first act of kindness and offer to help with the next. As the kind acts multiply, they attract more and more attention.

Most of us look at massive problems, such as poverty and homelessness, and are overwhelmed. This chapter is dedicated to those who have demonstrated the power of one.

9.2 Everyday Heroes

Scott van Duzer owns a Big Apple pizza shop in Fort Pierce, Florida. He became nationally-known when he gave President Barack Obama a bear hug during the 2012 presidential campaign. However, Scott had been widely-known in South Florida for some time. For example, when a young boy needed brain surgery at Boston Children's Hospital, Big Apple held a fund-raiser, with all the proceeds going toward travel expenses. When a firefighter died, leaving a wife and three children, he opened Big Apple for a fundraiser. Scott continues to hold these events and has established the van Duzer Foundation[138].

Most people visualize retirement as an opportunity to move to a warm climate, play golf, and sip martinis by the pool. Charlotte Tidwell, a retired nurse, saw it differently. She put herself on a tight budget and used the rest of her pension to fund a food pantry in her home town of Fort Smith, Arkansas. The city had been hit hard by plant closings, layoffs, and the recession. Her hard work and dedication inspired others to volunteer at the food pantry. They grew the project to serve seven thousand clients per month. Mrs. Tidwell said that she had been raised in a family and a church community that were dedicated to service. She has also identified a successor, in the event that she becomes unable to run the program. This is an important step for service entrepreneurs, because if it is neglected, the program may dissolve when the leader is no longer present[139].

Corinne Cannon was amazed by how expensive it was to raise an infant when her son Jack was born in 2009. Thinking how hard it must be for other new mothers who were less fortunate than

---

[138] http://www.vanduzerfoundation.org.
[139] NBC Nightly News, March 4, 2015.

herself to handle these expenses, she found out that diapers were not covered by food stamps or WIC funds. Searching for the nearest diaper bank, she found that there was not one established in Washington, D.C.

The D.C. Diaper Bank was founded in 2010 on her son's birthday to provide low-income families with access to diapers free of cost[140]. Corinne's organization is modeled after other diaper banks nationwide that provide diapers to social service agencies that help families. Diapers are a "gateway resource," getting hard-to-reach families in the door for other social services.

Since then, community response has be overwhelming, yielding donations from far and near. More than 500,000 diapers have been distributed throughout the District helping children under the age of three in low-income housing.

Corinne Cannon feels that there is a lot of work left to do to help people, but knowing that making lives better for babies and families all over the community is a heartwarming feeling for all involved. Corinne was nominated and became a finalist for the 2014 L'Oréal Women of Worth list.

One day in 1999, Jack Hairston saw a young man fall off his bicycle in front of his house in West Palm Beach, Florida. Although, he was disabled, Jack hobbled out to the street to help. He diagnosed the problem and fixed the bike. Soon other children in the neighborhood were bringing their broken bikes to Jack.

Jack's neighborhood was heavily populated with migrant workers from Guatemala. Many of these families could not afford to buy bicycles for their children. Jack began to collect broken bikes,

---

[140] http://www.dcdiaperbank.org.

repair and customize them, and give them to the poorest children. Volunteers from the neighborhood began to come over to help.

These acts of kindness allowed Jack and his volunteers to earn the trust and respect of the children. They became mentors to the children, helping them learn English, and assisting with their school assignments. WPTV noticed and did a report about Jack. This brought in more donations and volunteers from Fort Lauderdale to Vero Beach.

For Christmas in 2013, Jack and his cohort gave away over 900 bicycles. They expected to give away 1,400 in the 2014 Christmas season[141].

Besides becoming a local celebrity, Jack has derived other benefits from his work. He reports that focusing on the problems of others has helped to improve his health.

Brittany Hodak was filming an episode of the hit TV show Shark Tank when she got a phone call from a producer informing her that he had forgotten to give her a *per diem* check for her travel expenses. She thought that $65 per day was a generous amount for meals and that she wouldn't have missed it. Then she thought about the contrast between successful people who didn't need the assistance and the 20% of the population that were facing food uncertainty. Over Thanksgiving, she shared her thoughts with her cousin Jennifer Barker. When the two were growing up, they had dreamed of tackling a big project together, and they brainstormed about a program to transfer the funds to fight hunger. Per Diems Against Poverty was invented[142]. The organization channels donated *per diem* funds to Feeding America, which serves 46.5 million Americans in need. Its economies of scale allow it to

---

[141] http://jackthebikeman.org/about_us.
[142] http://www.perdiemsagainstpoverty.org

distribute a meal for as little as $0.10. Per Diems Against Poverty has established core values, two of which are integrity and frugality. Volunteers absorb overhead costs, so 100% of donations go to feeding the hungry. New York Mets outfielder Curtis Granderson is one of the celebrities who contributes his *per diem* checks.

In 2008 Jennie Dundas, 40-year-old co-owner of Brooklyn's socially conscious Blue Marble Ice cream shops (which use local organic milk and renewable energy), met Rwandan drummer and playwright Odile Gakire Katese at a theater workshop[143]. They got to talking about the 1994 genocide that killed 80,000 people and left Kateses' homeland in a seemingly permanent state of mourning. Katese had an idea.

"She thought an ice cream parlor would bring joy and indulgence, as well as empowerment through jobs," Dundas says. After raising $80,000 in grants and donations, Dundas's business partner, Alexis Miesen, 35, journeyed to Butare (pop. 90,000) to help train members of Kateses' all-women's Ingoma Nshya Drumming Cooperative. Most of these women scraped by with selling eggs or braiding hair in shop operations.

These days, with Dundas and Miesen's help, the drummers run an ice-cream parlor called Inzozi Nziza ("Sweet Dreams") which enables its 11employees to feed, clothe, and educate more than 70 family members. It also contributes to the livelihood of dozens of dairy farmers, coffee bean growers, and beekeepers.

Since about 90 percent of Rwanda lacks access to electricity, most customers have never tasted frozen treats. Homemade flavors like maracuja (passion fruit) "typically inspire amused shock," says Miesen. Eventually, the Rwandan women will assume full control

---

[143] http://www.bluemarbledreams.com.

of the business and Miesen says, "We'll cheer them on from the sidelines."

Sometimes an opportunity isn't a lucky break but the result of dedicated individual effort. As a judge in St. Louis Juvenile Court, Jimmie Edwards got frustrated by an endless parade of offenders through his courtroom. Together with 45 community partners, he founded Innovative Concept Academy in an abandoned school building[144]. Troubled young people were educated in an environment of strict discipline and intensive counseling. Many young people were able to finish high school and change the direction of their lives. As previously stated, a key goal is to increase the number of helpers and decrease the number of those needing help.

9.3 Celebrities Turn the Spotlight Around

As we've seen, anyone with enough thought and commitment can launch a program that can grow and affect the lives of thousands. However, celebrities can shine a bright light on a problem and/or solution. This focus can draw badly-needed resources, funds, and volunteers to a cause that is overwhelmed.

One example is Mary's Meals, a project dedicated to providing school meals to children in the poorest areas of the world[145]. The scope of this challenge is overwhelming; but the strategy is to empower each community to stand up on its own resources. When actor Gerard Butler became involved, CNN and other media took notice. Talent, attention, and dedication forged a powerful supporting force.

---

[144] a) People Magazine, Oct. 3, 2014; b)
www.innovativeonconceptacademy.com.
[145] http://www.marysmeals.org/.

Grammy award winner Jason Mraz has signed onto a project to turn around failing schools through the arts[146]. Being a creative individual, Mraz developed methods to teach grammar. For example, one song described the functions of helper verbs. One failing Burbank school saw a dramatic increase in attendance and test scores. Some other notable celebrities assisting are Forrest Whittaker, Carrie Washington, Marc Anthony, and Chad Smith. As noted throughout this book, the path to reducing poverty depends on the opportunity to learn and comprehend essential information and useful skills.

In 2005, New Orleans was devastated by Hurricane Katrina. The heaviest flooding was in the lower Ninth Ward, where the levee was breached by a runaway barge. The neighborhood was reduced to piles of mud and wreckage. Like the movie heroes he portrays, Brad Pitt came to rescue the neighborhood and founded Make It Right[147]. On the tenth anniversary of Katrina, 109 angular, brightly-painted homes stood as a fulfillment of the Make It Right commitment. This embodiment of recovery involved a collaboration of ecologists and experts in affordable construction. Enduring success is also assured by the participation of the returning residents on the type and décor of the houses.

Many athletes have escaped the poverty of inner city neighborhoods, based primarily by dedication to their physical skills. However, very few make it to the top of the professional sports world. A lot of headlines have shown the dark side of professional sports, like drug abuse, domestic violence, and even homicide. But there are sports heroes reaching back and helping the youth in their hometowns.

---

[146] http://www.today.com/video/today/56862406#57102258
[147] http://www.nola.com/katrina/index.ssf/2015/08/brad_pitt_feels.

175

LeBron James grew up in a single-parent household in Akron, Ohio. He was a natural on the court in high school, often scoring up to 100 points in a single game. In a rare transition, he skipped college and went directly into the NBA. He led the Miami Heat to two championships before returning to the Cleveland Cavaliers, determined to bring an elusive championship to that franchise.

James' heart was always in the northeast Ohio region where he grew up. He established the LeBron James Family Foundation, dedicated to improving the state of poor families[148]. LeBron has established a 41million dollar scholarship fund, in partnership with Akron University, to provide a path for Akron's kids from poor neighborhoods to attend college for four years[149]. The first graduates of the program are expected to receive their degrees in 2021.

One beloved celebrity can inspire generations of entrepreneurial philanthropists. Walter Payton was an all-star running back for the Chicago Bears. He was often seen walking around the Chicago area smiling and talking to his fans and the children. Following his death, the National Football League (NFL) established the Walter Payton Award, presented to an NFL player who distinguishes himself in humanitarian activity.

Anquan Boldin, the most recent Walter Payton Man of the Year, grew up in the Palm Beach County city of Pahokee. Boldin was a quarterback at Florida State and was drafted into the NFL and converted into an all-pro wide receiver, and played for the Arizona Cardinals, Baltimore Ravens, and the San Francisco 49ers.

---

[148] http://lebronjamesfamilyfoundation.org.
[149]http://www.foxsports.com/nba/story/lebron_james_college_scholarships_12/23/2015.

In 2012, he set a Ravens' single-season record for receptions and receiving yards, and was a key contributor to winning the Super Bowl.

To give back to the community, Boldin founded the Anquan Boldin Foundation[150]. The foundation, in cooperation with Florida Crystal, organized a summer enrichment program that offers high school students from Palm Beach County the opportunity to spend eight weeks catching up on their academic skills. The organization also created a scholarship program for students from Pahokee and the San Francisco Bay area. The foundation has awarded eight 4-year scholarships. Anquan also has been active in Oxfam America since 2010, accompanying two trips to Ethiopia and Senegal using his influence to lobby for Senegalese relief at the White House.

9.4 The Last Full Measure of Love

As the Bible says: "Greater love hath no man than to lay down his life for a friend." In wartime, we often hear stories of heroic acts, a soldier throws his body on a grenade or runs through live fire to aid a wounded comrade. We hear these stories, wondering and hoping that we would have that much courage in such a desperate event. But sometimes, individuals are performing peaceful acts of compassion, when their lives are taken unexpectedly.

---

[150] http://www.q81.org.

9.4.1 Students of Lynn University[151]

Britney Gengel was a 19-year old sophomore at Lynn University in Boca Raton, Florida. She volunteered to go to Haiti to help hand out food to hungry children. The project was sponsored by Florida-based Food for the Poor. Britney was appalled at the plight of orphans in the country, and wrote to her parents that she wanted to return to build an orphanage[152].

On January 12, 2010, a magnitude 7.0 earthquake devastated the impoverished country. The Haitian government estimated the death toll at 300,000 and the homeless at 1.5 million. The hotel where the Lynn University students were staying collapsed. After 33 days of searching, rescuers reported the heartbreaking news that Britney, three other students, and two faculty members had been killed.

The grief-stricken Gengel family remembered Britney's dream. Len Gengel, Britney's father and a construction professional, committed himself to building an orphanage. Len designed the building in the shape of a "B." It was flexible but sturdy; the type of building that can resist earthquakes and hurricanes. After many trips to Haiti, the orphanage was opened. It houses 33 girls and 33 boys, the exact number of days that Britney laid under the rubble of the hotel. It costs $75,000 to run the orphanage. The expenses are borne by donations and volunteers. Currently, there are 300 donors giving $33 a month to sponsor a child.

---

[151] a) http://www.sun-sentinel.com/local/palm-beach/ap-fau-student-haiti, b) http:abcnews.go.com/topkics/news/lynn-university-haiti.htm, c) http://www.lyn.edu/haiti.
[152] L. Gengel, et al., *Heartache and Hope in Haiti: The Britney Gengel Story: Making Our Daughter's Last Wish Come True*, Second Edition, TriMark Press, 2013.

For its part, Lynn University established a Plaza of Remembrance on March 16, 2012 for students to reflect on the inspirational lives of Britney, Stephanie Crispinelli, Courtney Hayes, Christine Gianacaci, Patrick Hartwick, and Richard Bruno[153].

9.4.2 Tracy Biletnikoff

Like far too many young people, Tracy Biletnikoff, daughter of legendary Hall of Fame wide receiver Fred Biletnikoff, experimented with drugs and became addicted to heroin and methamphetamine. She sought treatment in the San Francisco Bay area, where she met Mohammed Harun Ali, who was also recovering from an addiction. Upon recovery, they both became counselors, helping other young addicts. Tracy became concerned about their relationship when Ali became controlling and abusive. When he confessed to her that he had relapsed, she confronted him and he strangled her to death[154]. After being convicted in two trials, Ali was sentenced to life in prison.

The Biletnikoff family was devastated by this profound tragedy and couldn't process what had happened to the wonderful girl whose life had been cut off at the age of 20. After several months of grieving, Fred and his wife Angela founded the Tracy Biletnikoff Foundation, dedicated to helping young girls to recover from addiction and abusive relationships[155]. The Biletnikoffs often visit Tracy's House of Hope, a 3-bedroom home east of Sacramento, where six teenage girls reside. They have trod the same path as Tracy - drugs, gangs, and domestic violence, but now are excitedly working on putting their lives back together.

---

[153] http://www.lynn.edu/haiti/in_remembrance/britney_gengel.
[154] http://www.articles.latimes.com/2000/may07/sports.
[155] http://biletnikoff.org.

9.4.3 Acts of Compassion vs. Acts of Terror

For the last four years, a bloody civil war has been raging in Syria. Estimates are that over 300,000 have been killed and over one million have become refugees. Kayla Mueller, a resident of Prescott, Arizona, was distressed by the suffering of the children in Syria and decided to get involved. She joined a Danish organization for refugees and left for Syria in 2012. On August 4, 2013 Kayla was captured by ISIS terrorists in Aleppo, as she left a hospital run by Doctors without Borders[156]. On July 4, 2014, United States Special Forces raided an ISIS stronghold in Raqqa in an attempt to rescue Kayla and three other American hostages. Unfortunately, they had been moved to another location.

In early February 2015, the U. S. Government and Kayla's family received information that Kayla had been killed. ISIS claimed that she had died in a Jordanian air strike. Pentagon sources denied this claim because there were no indications that air strikes had been carried out at that location.

The Mueller family, residents of Prescott, and Kayla's co-workers mourned her death. Her life could be described through two of her quotes. In a letter written to her father in 2011, she wrote: "I find God in the suffering eyes reflected in mine. If this is how you are revealed to me, this is how I will forever seek you." While in captivity, she wrote to her family: "I have a lot of fight left in me. I am not breaking down, plus I will not give in, no matter how long it takes." Kayla's legacy is her commitment to suffering people, especially children, and her total commitment to her faith. President Obama reacted to Kayla's death by saying: "On this day, we take comfort in the fact the future belongs not to those

---

[156] http://www.foxnews.com/world/2015/02/10/family_us_aid_worker_isis....

who destroy, but rather to the irrepressible force of human goodness that Kayla Mueller shall forever represent."

9.5 In Summary

Millions of people voluntarily give their time and money to help those who are less fortunate. Only a few lose their lives in this effort; but those who do, inspire many others. If we embrace the concepts of Compassionate Capitalism, we can add millions more to assisting those who struggle. Perhaps we will realize that government is not the first responder to hunger, homelessness, and illiteracy. We are! Of course, government can maintain a safety net, but we are closest to the problem.

Chapter 10

Where We Are and Where We Are Going

"Try to be a rainbow in someone's cloud."
-*Maya Angelou*-

10.1 Introduction -- How It's Already Happening

Businesses and wealthy businessmen have been carrying out charitable programs for many years. Even back in the industrial age, philanthropists like Andrew Carnegie have supported social, educational, and cultural activities. The sum total of all these *ad hoc* activities was to improve societies wherever they were implemented. The only things lacking were coordination and a name. Compassionate Capitalism can serve to fill in the voids, as fine cement particles fill in voids in an aggregate.

Entrepreneurs, partnerships, and corporations can leverage their employee's volunteerism to magnify and humanize their monetary contributions. United Way partners with businesses to solicit contributions from employees to fund local organizations. Only 10% of contributions have been used for salaries and expenses. United Way has had some problems raising funds because of the large number of causes it supports. Some donors have withheld their contribution because they objected to one or more causes listed on the United Way's brochure. For example, pro-life donors refused to give to medical facilities that performed abortions. There was also controversy over the Boy Scouts' refusal to admit gay scouts and scoutmasters.

In the 1990s, Kraft Foods decided to replace the United Way with an internally managed charitable organization known as the Kraft Employees' Fund. Employees were encouraged to submit local charities, which were selected by a committee. This internal effort channeled 100% of contributions to the local charities. This program evolved into the Kraft Foods Foundation, where the emphasis is on fighting hunger.

Some purist capitalists see no value to businesses contributing to social programs. They usually claim that the organization is distracted from its goal to make a profit for the shareholders.

Compassionate Capitalism would view it differently. Contributions of money and personnel are completely voluntary. Companies derive a number of advantages when they engage in the improvement of their communities:

- Feeding, clothing, and educating children in the communities result in young adults that may regard the company as their friend. These individuals become new consumers and employees for the company.

- As the humanitarian efforts of the company become known, it gains a good reputation in the community, except for a few cynics.

Gerard L. Hasenhuettl

- When employees become involved, their self-esteem rises. They also become the face of the company in the community.

- The community improvement projects serve as team building activities with a purpose, rather than those perpetrated by management consultants.

Of course, the macro goal of Compassionate Capitalism is to shift the numbers of people living in poverty toward happily-working people who can support themselves. This will result in a greater focus on those who are incapable of working and supporting themselves (the involuntary poor). Chapter 11 will suggest a strategy for implementing such programs. This chapter will concentrate on examples of what some companies are doing.

10.1.1 Feeding the Hungry

Food and water are staples for sustaining life. One can survive with shabby clothes or homelessness, in a safe location with a hospitable climate. Unfortunately, hunger is a worldwide problem. In undeveloped countries, some people actually starve to death. A more insidious problem is that lack of proper nutrition weakens the body and makes people more susceptible to viruses, bacteria, and parasites. Compounding the problem is the disruption of supply channels in theaters of war. Children are particularly vulnerable, since their immune systems may not be fully developed. They also need to be satiated with a reasonably balanced diet in order to learn. The United Nations, religious charities, and other non-governmental agencies are working hard to address the problem, but crossing combat lines is quite hazardous.

Developed countries rarely have people actually starving, but there are other nutritional problems. In poor areas, which often have high crime rates, there are fewer food stores. These areas are known as food deserts. It is counter-intuitive that obesity is a problem in these food deserts. There are a few reasonable explanations. People who have experienced hunger and uncertainty are psychologically driven to overeat when food is available. Many of both chain and independent restaurants in poor areas serve foods that are high in fat, sugar, and total calories. These types of foods have been labeled as junk, although they have a place in a balanced diet. Community groups and government nutritionists are making efforts to introduce more fruits and vegetables into the food deserts to properly balance the diet.

School lunch programs are common for low-income neighborhoods. Supervised by the USDA, these programs are trying to give children at least one balanced meal on school days. Some school systems have even expanded their programs into the weekends and summer months. One nagging problem with school lunches is that they are often incompatible with adolescent tastes. If foods do not taste good, they are more likely to be thrown in the waste cans than to be eaten.

Kraft Foods Foundation looked at the problem of food deserts and took action. In cooperation with Feeding America and local community groups, Kraft began to assist food pantries across the country. In addition to donating food products, the company initiated efforts to solve another problem. Residents in food deserts often have no available transportation to go to the food pantries. Kraft began to donate refrigerated food trucks to pantries in cities where there was inadequate transportation. Perishable foods could be transported into feeding centers located in churches and community centers. For example, the Treasure Coast in South Florida is spread out over a large area and bus services are operated by the individual counties. A truck allows the Treasure Coast Food Bank to move donated food into neighborhoods that had previously been underserved.

The Kraft Foods Foundation also encourages employees to volunteer to help community improvement efforts. Team leaders meet regularly to brainstorm and set goals for their teams. The benefit to employees is that they can sharpen their creative problem-solving skills. The company benefits when their employees bring their creativity and problem-solving skills back into the workplace.

People who cannot afford food have occasionally resorted to a practice known as "dumpster diving" at supermarkets. The food stores have been caught up in a modern dilemma. Their lawyers have undoubtedly told them that allowing this practice exposes the company to risk if someone should get sick on the discarded food. One creative store has allowed employees to bring out bags and boxes permitting people to "intercept" the food before it hits the dumpster. Sometimes, saving someone's dignity is as important as feeding them.

The human body can survive weeks or months without food. However, after several days without water, the body will become dangerously dehydrated. In a desperate search for water, people may drink from seriously contaminated sources. After natural disasters, such as hurricanes, floods, and earthquakes, it is critical to deliver large quantities of potable water to the affected areas. Bottling companies, such as Coca-Cola and Anheuser-Busch, have contributed their resources to these crises. In Flint, Michigan, the water was contaminated with lead after the city switched its source to the Flint River. Four of the largest bottled water companies stepped up to deliver water to the city's children, the most at-risk population.

10.1.2 Helping the Poorly Clothed

Over the millennia, humans have developed clothing to protect them from the cold and defend their sense of modesty. Gradually, clothing evolved into an indicator of status. Today brands like Armani, Gucci, and Rolex have risen to the top of the status heap. Even casual and sportswear have a brand hierarchy.

Unfortunately many across the world do not have enough discretionary income to purchase enough clothing and are forced to wear worn-out apparel. Organizations like the Salvation Army help distribute donated items. Private companies are also helping.

Tom's Shoes is a company that was founded with an embedded mission[157]. For every pair of shoes they sell, a pair is donated to someone who is indigent. To date, Tom's has given away over one million pairs of shoes. The company markets mainly in the United States and Europe, but its donations are spread worldwide. It has expanded its product line to include sunglasses, handbags, and apparel, which are included in the one-for-one program. Tom's has also gone beyond one-for-one and expanded its giving into other areas. For example, the company has formed partnerships that have reduced fluke worm infection in over two million children. Tom's has captured the essence of Compassionate Capitalism.

Other companies have also adopted the one-for-one model. Skyline Socks gives away a free pair for every pair sold in the local community[158]. For every pair of glasses sold by Warby Parker, the company donates the equivalent cost to non-profits

---

[157] http://www.toms.com.
[158] http://www.buzzfeed.com/jessicaprobus/23-charitable-companies-that-give-back.

worldwide[159]. In addition, Warby Parker contributes toward training locals to give eye exams. A Port Saint Lucie Wal-Mart added a personal touch to a back-to-school sale. Employees chartered buses to transport 90 children from Indiantown, and gave each child a new pair of shoes. For each item of clothing or backpack purchased from Oak, the company donates one backpack to a child at a homeless or at-risk shelter[160].

10.1.3 Sheltering the Homeless

Taking care of those that are homeless has been a problem that has traditionally been taken care of by governments and charitable organizations. In previous chapters, we have noted the activities of the Federal Government, the Salvation Army, and Habitat for Humanity. Private businesses should not feel left out, because there are many ways they can help. Of course, they can contribute money to homeless charities. They can also assist, through employee volunteers, to help educate, teach job skills, and share financial literacy knowledge. In the 1990s, the Maxwell House division of Kraft Foods launched their "Build 100" program. The goal was to sponsor Habitat to build 100 houses for low-income families. The company provided funding for materials, and local Kraft employees rotated in to supply labor. Local governments donated vacant lots or properties that were foreclosed for delinquent taxes. The city benefits by exchanging a non-taxpaying property for one that will pay.

Some companies use the one-for-one formula to contribute to shelters for the homeless. For example, for each comforter sold, The Company Store will donate one to a homeless child in the

---

[159] http://www.warbyparker.com.
[160] http://www.oaklifestyles.com.

United States[161]. For every item of winter clothing purchased from Twice as Warm, one will be donated to a local shelter[162].

Companies that do not have sufficiently high margins to initiate a one-for-one program can begin more modestly. Build-A-Bear Workshop is a highly innovative company that allows children to customize their own stuffed animal. At checkout, the customer is asked to identify their favorite charity and Build-a-Bear will contribute 5% of the sale to that charity. To date, the company has contributed over $25 million to a number of causes. Stuffed with Hugs is another outreach effort of Build-A-Bear. The Workshop donates stuffed animals to needy children around the world. More than 325,000 toys have been stuffed and donated. Build-A-Bear has lent a paw to causes such as children's health, childhood literacy, and social services through the Build-A-Bear Workshop Foundation.

This remarkable company was founded and led by Maxine Clark, a remarkable individual. She has received many personal awards, as has the Company, such as Forbes 100 Best Companies to Work For, three years in a row[163]. Ms. Clark and her husband were founding donors to KIPP Inspire Academy, a chain of charter schools with an innovative curriculum.

10.1.4 Healing the Sick

Medical care in the early twentieth century was centered on the family doctor. There were only basic medications and not many people were hospitalized. Recovery from serious conditions, such as heart disease and cancer, was not expected. Fast forward to the twenty-first century and there is an enormous arsenal of

---

[161] http://www.thecompanystore.com.
[162] http://www.twiceaswarm.com.
[163] See Forbes, Feb. 8, 2010.

medications used to treat serious diseases. Very complex surgeries are performed in hospitals and less serious procedures are done in outpatient facilities. Unfortunately, the pressures on doctors, hospitals, and health professionals have increased significantly. People expect to get well, no matter how serious the disease. Costs of care have risen at multiples of the rate of inflation. Consequently, many people cannot afford medical care for their diseases.

Primary care physicians often charge in excess of $100 per visit. The indigent often go to the emergency room for their care, since an ER cannot turn away patients who are unable to pay. However, an ER is designed to respond to emergencies, not primary care. A few tests may be performed to ensure that the condition is not life-threatening, and the patient is released without a plan of treatment. A better strategy for primary care is needed.

The HANDS Clinic, in Fort Pierce, Florida, is charged with providing primary care free to the indigent. Doctors and dentists volunteer to work at the clinic for several hours or a day. Other expenses are covered by Medicaid, donations, or government grants. The need for care is great, so the clinic is often crowded, but the wait is worth the competent care.

Hospitals have much more expensive physical facilities and cannot afford to give large amounts of free care. Traditionally, these costs have been shifted to patients who are insured. This practice has resulted in hospital bills that appear to be ridiculously high, but the indigent do receive their care. Unfortunately, some costs are not easily overcome. Take the case of an uninsured worker who was the victim of a hit-and-run driver. The man was treated in a hospital ER and admitted with a severe head trauma. He remained in a coma for more than a year. This was an enormous drain on the hospital's budget, but everyone stepped up to help. Nurses voluntarily worked shifts without being paid. In the end the man was transferred to a hospital in his home country. The man's family sued the hospital for initiating the transfer. Even though the suit was not successful, the legal costs were another body blow for the budget.

Hospital care is an area where successful people have stepped forward to help for many years. Some have been celebrities. Comedian Danny Thomas funded Saint Jude Medical Center in Nashville, where children with cancer can go for treatment, regardless of their ability to pay. Actress Frances Langford willed a large sum to Martin Memorial Hospital to upgrade their cardiac center. Successful business executives also came forward, sometimes in response to crises in their own families. John Huntsman established the Huntsman Cancer Center, and vowed to eliminate cancer from the world. It was a very ambitious goal and it was personal. Other examples include the Langone Medical Center and M. D. Anderson Hospital.

Advocacy of prominent people is beneficial in other ways. Respect for these individuals confers credibility on the institutions they endow. People in crisis may seek care at a medical facility they know. Others may make generous contributions to a fundraising effort, based on the reputation of the benefactor. This also puts a heavy responsibility on the institution to maintain this respect and to strive for perfection.

Prices for prescription drugs have risen almost exponentially over the past several decades. Drug companies have become villains in the theater of politics. They are accused of being greedy, caring more about profits than saving lives. Urban legends have sprung up about large companies suppressing natural cures to protect their franchises. In reality, the problem is more complex:

Older drugs have been relatively simple small molecules, assembled through convergent synthetic processes. Modern drugs are much more complex, requiring very complicated preparation and quality assurance tests.

Regulatory approvals are involved and time consuming processes. Estimated cost of developing a new drug range from $2.6-4.0 billion[164].

Many new drugs fall out during clinical trials due to unacceptable toxicity or insufficient effectiveness. These costs are spread over the successful candidates.

Countries with national health care systems negotiate lower prices with drug companies. Costs are shifted to U.S. patients, similar to the practice in hospitals. The high prices subsidize the high costs of R&D.

Recently, the time for approval of many generic drugs have been slower in the FDA. Companies must prove that the generic drugs are equivalent for safety and effectiveness.

It will be quite difficult to solve the problem of high drug prices without sacrificing R&D and drug availability (remember the law of supply and demand), drug safety, and the existence of profitable and innovative drug companies. Improving the efficiency of drug discovery, clinical trials, and approval processes would be helpful. Wellness programs with balanced nutrition and more physical activity will be helpful. There is also need for more cures and fewer maintenance drugs.

---

[164] a)
http://www.forbes.com/sites/matthewherper/2012/02/10/the_truly_staggering_c ost_of_inventing_new_drugs, b) Milman, J., The Washington Post: Nov. 18, 2014.

Mental health is an area of medical care that is bordering on a crisis. Until the 1970s, people with mental conditions could be locked up in a mental facility without their consent. Following a Supreme Court decision, waves of patients were released back into their communities. It was generally agreed that they would receive better care in a familiar environment. Unfortunately, this was an academic theory that fell short in the real world. Many of these former patients joined the swelling ranks of the homeless. Recently, there has been a cluster of mass shootings by individuals who appear to have serious mental conditions.

Like many social problems, several causes can be identified:

- There is an historical stigma attached to mental illness, possibly bred from a fear of the unknown or perhaps the Bible stories of demonic possession. Consequently, both patients and their families have a tendency toward denial. Parents fear that a child with mental problems will be labeled.

- The brain is the most complicated organ in the body and therefore the least understood. Conditions, symptoms, and their diagnostic codes seem to be increasing exponentially.

- Like the conditions, diagnoses are very complex and vulnerable to error. Can variations in behavior be defined as multiple disorders or can a single disease manifest in different ways?

- Like most prescription drugs, side effects can occur. If these are unpleasant, patients will resist taking their medications.

Solutions to such a complicated problem are elusive, the causes described above are not only complex, they are also interactive.

193

Many voices are demanding that governments need to spend more money to correct the problem. But if we have trouble defining the solutions, where do we allocate the money? Certainly more basic research is required to understand how the chemistry of the brain affects behavior. This will help drug companies to design effective treatments with fewer side effects. Maybe the first question to ask is how an anti-depressive can increase the risk of suicide. If there is a shortage of mental health professionals, we can train more or use existing resources more efficiently. Let's also ask the question: How far do we go to find problems? Maybe some of us are just a little odd.

Mental health is an area where Compassionate Capitalism has room to operate. Drug companies are certainly drawn to a market that has high demand. They probably recognize that their present arsenal of maintenance drugs is insufficient. It will be interesting to see whether they will strive for a cure which has no side effect.

On the social front, a few brave celebrities have become advocates for mental health. There is a fear among agents and business managers that their clients could be tainted with the stigma that still surrounds mental illness.

10.1.5 Teaching the Children and Adults

The long range solution to poverty is to educate and train people so they can support themselves and their families. This can also be a step toward alleviating "income inequality." Even if there are no jobs available, an educated, trained, and enterprising person can find something to do for an income. Once they have earned the money, they should also know how to manage and invest it.

Teachers are some of the most valuable people in our economy, and accordingly, this book has been dedicated to them. Mothers are also included, since they are their children's first teachers. Excellent mothers and teachers know how to teach, but also inspire, motivate, and mentor. Unfortunately, they have been unfavorably treated by the supply-demand curve.

Companies can also perform valuable services for our struggling school systems. Of course, they can contribute money, equipment, and services. PNC Bank has pledged $1 million per year to support K-8 education. Bank employees can render another valuable service. A few banks in Chicago encouraged their employees to design creative and entertaining programs about financial literacy, then present them in the schools. Poor kids will listen and participate in projects that involve money, because they have so little of it. They can learn the difference between needs and wants, create a budget, manage their bank accounts, learn how to shop for a loan, and how to avoid being swindled.

The Big Shoulders Fund was founded in 1986 by a group of Chicago business and civic leaders with the encouragement of Joseph Cardinal Bernadin[165]. The fund contributes to inner-city Catholic schools that provide a quality values-based education. In addition to an annual $20 million dollar gift, executives volunteer their time to meet with children to encourage leadership development.

The Kraft Foods Technology Center adopted an elementary school on the west side of Chicago and presented creative hands-on science projects. Volunteers also came to the school on Saturdays to help children with their homework.

Companies can also assist students with career guidance. Many students give little thought to what they want to do when they graduate. They may take a wild guess as to what they think they

---

[165] http:www.bigshouldersfund.org.

would like to do, but they don't take the time to learn about the industry or the job. A hands-on project would involve creating a graph of jobs with two axes: jobs they would like and jobs they would be good at doing. Some career counselors feel they are done when the student has matched ability and interest. One more step is important. With some time in a library, a student can ferret out starting salaries for preferred jobs. Someone from a low-income family may not be happy with a low-paying job.

Whoever discovered the concept that learning is a lifelong experience was a very wise individual. Some brains don't mature as rapidly as others. In previous chapters we have proposed the concept of a "side door" to the education system. Life is like a train schedule. If you miss your train, you can catch the next one. Of course in both cases, you may have to pay a penalty. In education, it is measured in lost years of opportunity. Many colleges are recognizing that there are students that need to learn or review some basic prerequisites before proceeding. Siemens has formed partnerships with community colleges to customize programs for some of their new employees. Hammermill Paper founded in 1898 by four members of the Behrend family, established scholarships for working adults and employees' children[166]. The company endowed a learning center east of Erie, PA, which would become the Behrend Campus of Pennsylvania State University.

When Hammermill was acquired by International Paper, the fund was transferred to an entity that continued the scholarships[167]. These two companies are examples of the paternal spirit of German companies.

---

[166] See M. Mcquillan, *The Best Known Name in Paper: Hammermill: A History of the Company, Hammermill Paper Co., 1985.*
[167] Unpublished source.

The Dwarf Grill, predecessor of Chick Fil-A, was founded by Truett Cathy in 1946 in Hapeville, Georgia[168] . It was originally a full-service restaurant. The current fast-food franchise has over 1,950 stores. Chick-Fil-A has a scholarship fund available to employees and encourages them to develop their background[169]. Each student is provided at least $4,000 annually. Total annual assistance is $1.6 million and, to date, the company has contributed over $30 million. One student received a degree in nutrition from Florida State University. Her seven years of experience at Chick-Fil-A helped her get an internship. This company is an example of a career path from entry level through higher education.

Sometimes people make life-altering mistakes. Rehabilitation programs are available to mitigate the damage. Volunteers from some private companies visit prisoners to teach skills that will assist them to turn their lives around. Unfortunately, these programs vary widely among the prisons for availability and quality.

10.2 Miscellany

New York is one of the wealthiest cities in the world, yet about 1.8 million people live in poverty. In 1988, billionaire hedge fund manager Paul Tudor Jones founded the Robin Hood Foundation[170]. The Foundation recruited wealthy New Yorkers to engage in a massive effort to reduce poverty in the city. Over its nearly 25-year history, the organization has raised over $1.25 billion, of which 100% went to poverty-fighting programs. Childhood health and education was a critical component. It was

---

[168]http://www.businessinsider.com/chick_fil_a_history_and_facts_2016_1.
[169] http://www.chick-fil-a.com/Company/Responsibility_Giving/Youth_and_Education_Programs.
[170] https://en.wikipedia.org/Robin_Hood_Foundation.

as simple as providing health support, like inhalers to children with asthma, who had fewer absences from school. The story of Robin Hood was that he stole from the rich and gave to the poor. The Foundation approaches the rich and convinces them to willingly give to the poor. This is the vision of Compassionate Capitalism.

Shake Shack was founded initially as a food cart in New York by restaurateur Danny Meyer[171]. Located in Madison Square Park, the cart served Angus beef burgers, New York-style hot dogs, French fries, and their highly-acclaimed milkshakes. Meyer recruited his employees from the ranks of the long-term unemployed. They were taught to prepare a perfect burger one at a time. Men and women, who felt down and out, were able to recover their self-esteem by becoming passionate about preparing Shake Shack food. The company recently became public and is rapidly expanding both nationally and globally. Employees will have opportunities to advance.

Youth unemployment is a very stubborn problem in urban areas. The causes are often complex and difficult to remediate. Many urban children are raised by single parents. The parents may be working multiple jobs to support the family. Drugs and gangs are huge problems in many inner city neighborhoods. All these negative factors act as a drag on the local school systems. The result is that too many children are not provided the education and skills they need to be successful.

When Gerald Chertavian was a recent college graduate, he volunteered to become a big brother. Through this interaction he was disturbed that his younger brother was so poorly equipped for a successful career. In the year 2000, Gerald founded the Year Up

---

[171] a) https://en/wikipedia.org/wiki/Shake-Shack; b) http://www.shakeshack.com. https://en/wikipedia.org/

program in Boston[172]. The organization places young urban adults, ages 18-24, into companies where they receive job training, college credit, corporate internships, and support. Expectations for the young people are set high, but the level of support is also high. Year Up has expanded into several other U. S. cities and, to date, Year Up has served over 10,000 students. The organization has received a 4-star rating from Charity Navigator for 10 consecutive years.

The point to be made in this chapter is to show that many businesses are already practicing the tenet of placing a priority on the poor. The way forward is for other companies to become enlightened, not through force, but through the realization that helping the poor is the right thing to do.

---

[172] http://www.yearup.org.

Chapter 11

Strategies to Implement Compassionate Capitalism

"A journey of a thousand miles begins with a single step."
-Chinese philosopher Laozi, 604 B.C.-

11.1 Introduction --Where to Begin?

The above quote goes right to the heart of the problem of initiating any program. As authors know well, the hardest part of writing a novel is writing the first sentence. So it also goes with a strategy to help the poor. The problem is so enormous and multi-faceted that it is difficult to find a place to start. It is easier for a sole proprietor. Scott van Duzer simply saw someone who was in trouble and dedicated his pizza restaurant to a one- day fundraiser. Of course, as a small business, he risked decreasing his bottom line. In a partnership, one person has to convince the other partners on which project to tackle, how much time to commit, and which resources to apply. A corporation also answers to its shareholders and its board of directors who represent them. Some purist financial pundits believe that businesses should not be responsible for correcting social problems. They seem to yearn for the return to the rapacious capitalism of the Industrial Age.

A logical first step is to simply look around. Strategic planners will recognize this step as a situation analysis. What is the situation in the communities where your company is located? What is the unemployment rate, the degree of homelessness, the crime rate, and the quality of the schools? Now turn the telescope around and look inside your company. What is your core business? What are the skills and interests of your managers and employees? Are some of them already involved with volunteer projects?

The next step is to compare the two views you have just analyzed. Are there any areas that seem to match up? This step corresponds to the SWOT (strengths, weaknesses, opportunities, and threats) analysis. It is also where leverage points are identified. Kraft knew that it was a global food company. It was natural that they were capable of leading a fight against hunger in their communities. The Kraft Foods Foundation sharpened its focus on the problem.

If there is an obvious match, are there any organizations that your company could join to form a joint venture? For example, the Kraft Foods Foundation teamed up with Feeding America. A partnership offers the opportunity to brainstorm for new creative approaches.

11.2 Building a Durable Effort

Anyone who has been in a corporate career knows how quickly priorities can change when top management is reorganized. It is disheartening to start a program to help people in need, only to have top management shut it down. The company also loses credibility in the communities it abandons. Before committing to a

Compassionate Capitalism program, top management should implant their values into the fiber of the company's core values. The Mission Statement could contain a phrase explicitly making a commitment to the community. If this is impractical, the statement should be enshrined into the core values of the company.

The strategy should continue to develop ideas to attack the problem. Then tactics, resources, and timing should be defined. Consideration should be given to how rapidly the charitable effort can grow. Growing it too slowly can be discouraging. Growth that is too rapid may overwhelm even a large company. The plan should have the same time horizon as the rest of the company's strategic plans. This will help establish the program as a permanent part of the company's mission.

Perhaps the most important part of the planning process is the selection of a community partner and listening carefully to their input. Since the partner is closer to the problem, they need to share their views on strategy and tactics. Conversations may also result in innovative solutions that neither side has considered.

11.3 Fueling the Fire

Picking employees to run the physical program should be given serious thought because the human element is the most important factor for success. Managers who are good at driving production may not be the best candidates to deal with compassion, but then, you might be surprised. There is a risk that you might lose a very dedicated employee. Some feel it is more rewarding to help the poor, than to make widgets. The best the company can do is to release them with love and wish them good luck.

Volunteer employees are generally enthusiastic and pleasant when performing their charitable work. This is an unmeasurable good, since they are the face of the company to the community. Team leaders are important. They are coaches and observers. The leaders can identify strengths and weaknesses that line managers have not noticed. Communication with line management may identify a path for advancement in the organization for the employee with the newly-discovered talent.

11.4 The Chief Compassion Officer

Many expressions exist that say in many ways that leadership begins at the top. One of these is from President Harry Truman: "The buck stops here." Even if the idea rises from the grass-roots level, it needs to be approved at the top, if it is to be a lasting success. The continuity of a compassionate program depends on the continued support of the CPO. If a program fails, the company suffers a loss of credibility in the community.

Continued support is more difficult to achieve in a public corporation, since the tenure of management is dependent on the approval of the shareholders and the board of directors. Of course, if the CEO is a majority shareholder, the odds are tilted in his/her favor. This is often the case with company founders, although Steve Jobs was deposed by the board of Apple Computer. John Huntsman and Mark Zuckerberg have already been mentioned earlier as examples of dedication to worthy causes. Bill Gates retired as CEO of Microsoft to spend more time with his family and the Bill and Melinda Gates Foundation[173]. The Foundation funds projects worldwide to promote education, agricultural development, financial services for the poor, and improving global health. It is supporting vaccine projects and funding

---

[173] http://www.gatesfoundation.org.

research on diseases such as pneumonia, tuberculosis, malaria, HIV, and enteric diseases.

Gates also recruited billionaire Warren Buffett, CEO of investment company Berkshire-Hathaway, to join in his charitable activities[174]. Buffett pledged $30.7 billion in Berkshire stock to the Gates Foundation. He also intends to leave 99% of his estate to charity.

Michael Bloomberg, former CEO of Bloomberg Financial and ex-mayor of New York, has established a foundation which has a myriad of charitable objectives. For example, he contributed $53 million to increase fish populations in Brazil, Chile, and the Philippines. Other causes were smoking cessation, prevention of drowning deaths, and urban innovation.

---

[174] http://www.forbes.com/profile/warren_buffett.

Chapter 12

A Special Challenge to the Financial Community

"I have always been afraid of banks."
-Andrew Jackson-

12.1 Defining Problems

For the last decade, we have begun to see changes in the way work gets done in the United States. While most people are still employed full-time, others have seen their roles shift to contract labor, part-time work, or taking a part-time job to supplement inadequate wages from a full-time job. This has been described as "the gig economy." Change always offers challenges as well as opportunities. Some may be exhilarated by the control they have on their work schedule. Spouses may stagger their schedules to accommodate their need for child care. The challenges are that these types of work are often irregular (feast or famine) and there are no health or pension benefits.

Examples may be found in the construction industry as contract labor or in the "sharing economy" as with Uber or Aire B&B. The latter category is inextricably linked to intelligent hardware and software. Steve Case has described the skills to deal with the changing work patterns[175]. An entrepreneur needs to be able to handle stress, since there is a great deal of uncertainty. He/she needs to be an early adopter of technology, but tolerate the risks of doing so. If the venture is successful, there is great satisfaction in charting one's own course.

12.2 The Entrepreneur's Problem

Once the economic environment is set for innovation (economic and personal freedom), the next ingredient is a supply of entrepreneurs. They are energetic people who transform innovations into marketable products. In order to do this, they need to invest capital into start-up location, materials, and services. If the entrepreneur is wealthy, obtaining the necessary capital is not necessarily a problem. However, a poor entrepreneur has historically not had access to this capital.

Banks have been very reluctant to invest in entrepreneurial start-ups, because of their high risks. They base this reluctance on the statistics that show high failure rates of new businesses. Poor people do not have substantial collateral to pledge toward a loan. Often the business is just an idea with no track record. The entrepreneur may have no education or training in how to run a business.

Large banks have been uninterested in small businesses, which they have indicated by requiring substantial minimum balances to qualify for "free" checking. Fortunately, this problem can easily be solved by dealing with a community bank or credit union.

---

[175] S. Case, *The Third Wave*, Simon & Schuster, 2016.

However if a small firm does business that involves foreign currency transactions, a large bank may be essential.

Start-ups may also be overwhelmed by government regulations. On the federal level, IRS, Labor Department, OSHA, EPA, and EEOC may have hundreds or thousands of pages of rules that must be obeyed. State and local governments also demand compliance with their regulations. A recent trend has been to merge counties around metropolitan areas to form regional authorities. Large corporations retain accountants, lawyers, and regulatory experts to deal with these problems. Small businesses lack these resources and are at a competitive disadvantage.

12.3 Pioneering a Solution

Solutions in the past meant relying on a wealthy relative, saving toward an initial investment, or borrowing from an unscrupulous character. Most poor people do not have a wealthy relative. Those who do may have difficulty selling their idea. Saving is very difficult, especially if the poor person has a family. Borrowing from a loan shark may lead to an undesirable partnership or loss of the entire business.

As with many other problems, innovators are beginning to enter the financial field. Angel investors, private capital managers, and even popular TV shows are popularizing these new sources. Regardless, the entrepreneur needs to practice due diligence before going ahead.

12.3.1 A Mellow Miracle

A college student working in a pizza shop to earn spending money is not a rare phenomenon. Two students at Georgia Tech took pride in the quality of the products and developed ideas on how they could be improved. After borrowing some family money, they opened a pizza restaurant just off the Georgia Tech campus. Students liked their pizzas and hoagies, and lines began to form outside the small storefront. After a few years, they began to expand their business throughout the Atlanta area, then throughout the state. New locations were strategically located near colleges. Customers expressed interest in opening franchises. Today, the company has spread through the Southeast, with a couple locations in the West. Franchise prices range from $1.2-4 million. This example illustrates the power of committed entrepreneurs.

12.3.2 Financing Peace

Muhammad Yunus was a professor of economics, who had received his Ph.D. in the United States. In 1972, he returned to the newly-independent country of Bangladesh, joining the faculty of Chittagong University. Professor Yunus began working with the poor to improve their economic status. He noticed that poor entrepreneurs were not able to get bank loans and had to deal with private firms that charged outrageous interest rates. He began to guarantee bank loans for the banks and ended up founding the Gramen Bank, specializing in micro loans to the poor. The bank's borrowers grew to 7 million, 97% of whom were women. All loans were made using funds from the bank's depositors. The delinquency rate on these loans was miniscule, confirming Yunnus' faith in these people.

In 2006 Muhammad Yunus was awarded the Nobel Peace prize for pioneering the practice of micro loans[176]. He has received

---

[176] http://www.nobelprize.org/nobel_prizes/peace/laureates/2006/yunus.

numerous other awards and honors in Bangladesh and in many countries. He is also the author of two highly-regarded books[177].

The practice of micro-lending has spread widely, but is still not a focus of large banks. This may be good because it is not one of their core competencies. Some financial companies have embraced the concept and have grown large through their profits. The New York Times has questioned the high interest rates, fees, and points that some of these firms have charged[178]. Muhammad Yunus commented: "We created microcredit to fight the loan sharks; we didn't create microcredit to encourage new loan sharks." Of course lending to the poor is considered high-risk; reporters have discovered that some have charged as high as 125%. Risks are high largely because the poor have little education and experience in managing money and running a business.

In the United States, there are over 200 community organizations that specialize in micro-loans[179]. Most of them are nonprofit. A critical part of their services is the education and advice they provide. Their rates are low because they receive support from government agencies, mainly the Small Business Administration (SBA). The entrepreneurs benefit from the training and are more likely to succeed. This improves the prospects that the company will be paid back. The government benefits by receiving tax payments from another successful business. It's a perfect win-win-win scenario.

---

[177] a) M. Yunus and A. Jols, A. *Banker to the Poor: Micro-Lending and the Battle Against World Poverty*, Public Affairs, 2008; b) M. Yunus and K. Weber, *Creating a World Without Poverty: Social Business and the Future of Capitalism, Public Affairs, 2009.*
[178] N. MacFarquhar, The New York Times, April 13, 2010.
[179] a) http://www.entrepreneur.com/article/52724; b) Sheehy, K., http://www.nerdwallet.com/blog/small_business/ top_nonprofit_microfinance_lenders_in_the_us.

Gerard L. Hasenhuettl

Perhaps the best model for a prospective entrepreneur is to follow the Mellow Mushroom plan. They should work 1-2 years in the industry where they plan to start a business. They would learn whether they even like that industry. It would give them the opportunity to observe the processes, competitors, and supply chain. They could then obtain a micro-loan and build their business into profitability. Once they have a track record of success, they can graduate to a community bank. If they are wildly successful then they could open a relationship with a large bank, which could help if they are interested in expanding globally.

An alternative to debt financing for entrepreneurs is a sale of equity in the business. Venture capitalists are always searching for attractive business opportunities. Before attempting this route, the entrepreneur should seek competent financial and legal advice. The value of the business, the value the investor brings, and the control of the venture should be estimated. Only in exceptional circumstances should the entrepreneur give up controlling interest.

Specialized sources for funding are available online. Kick Starter is a crowd funding source that specializes in funding artistic and creative entrepreneurs[180].

This Cinderella story is illustrative of the many small businesses that were started in the basement, garage, or kitchen. Today it is more difficult because of the maze of government regulations that an entrepreneur must untangle. In a recent interview, the founder of Home Depot stated that he would not be successful under current regulations. However, the entrepreneurial spirit believes that success is accomplished by persistence in the face of uncertainty.

---

[180] http://www.kickstarter.com.

EPILOG

Long ago, humans began to explore a world that was simultaneously hostile and supportive. Storms, weather extremes, and vicious predators were dangers. Edible plants and game were plentiful. There for the taking. The first of their kind had no laws, traditions, knowledge base, or technology. Progress and learning were slow in the prehistoric era. Over the millennia, they began to develop all of these attributes that we take for granted today. Innovation was there from the beginning. They learned to make weapons, gather food, and to get along with one another. Since there was no written tradition, we have only sketchy information about how it all happened.

Innovation advanced the standard of living for the human race, slowly at first, and then rapidly. New technologies bred other new technologies, both from logic and serendipity. It was a bipolar process, developing ways to heal and ways to kill. Reason and logic developed concepts of right or wrong.

Innovation and its diffusion occurred in waves. A new technology generated a frenzy of competition until a dominant design emerged. Then standardization began; the technology that was revolutionary became a commodity. Economies, to some extent, followed these waves. Price competition among commodities led to a search for cheaper raw materials and lower labor costs. Manufacturing moved to geographic areas where the supply of labor was higher. The economy limped along until the next innovation was born. Entrepreneurs cushioned the shock by inventing new applications or services for the newly-abundant commodity.

Innovators and entrepreneurs are vital to a nation's prosperity. To date, centrally planned economies have shown a fairly dismal record of encouraging these essential people. Capitalism has been an engine for economic activity, but rewards have been unevenly distributed. A rational approach is to allow capitalism to flourish and produce economic growth.

Compassionate Capitalism encourages innovation and entrepreneurship to achieve economic growth. Individuals and companies should be encouraged to help less fortunate individuals to enhance their skills and education to share in the prosperity. Faith communities have shown the path. Government has provided safety nets, but they must untangle the bureaucracies to maximize their efficiency or privatize these functions. Migration and severe financial crises bred sacrificial generations. Parents worked hard and lived frugally so their children could benefit from education and have a better life. Perhaps the economic collapse will stimulate another such generation.

Above all, everyone must seek to improve their integrity to simplify economic transactions. Individuals are free to conduct themselves in any legal fashion, but they must recognize the karma of social media. Individuals cannot be forced to succeed, but should not blame others for their failures. As we have seen, Compassionate Capitalism is already being practiced. If we can significantly expand it, we will approach the tipping point of equal opportunity.

APPENDIX A

THE COMPASSIONATE CAPITALIST
MANIFESTO

It is essential that an economic system is based on maximum personal and economic freedom. Enforcement of laws and regulations must protect these freedoms for all people. Freedom is only limited by the actions of one individual which negatively impact another individual.

Integrity is the core value of Compassionate Capitalism. Failure to adhere to integrity in all transactions will lead to more restrictive laws and regulations, which reduce efficiency and increase compliance costs in the economy.

Every individual has the right to obtain an education, compete for a job, and to start a business. Individual intellectual, physical, emotional, and moral development is essential for a thriving economy.

There must be a strong commitment to assist the involuntary poor to escape poverty and participate in society and the economy. This effort is the freely-accepted responsibility of individuals and businesses.

Individuals and businesses should join with communities to make them safe, clean, and areas of economic opportunity. The focus can then be widened to include larger areas.

APPENDIX B

ECONOMIC AND SOCIAL PRINCIPLES AND ANALOGIES TO SCIENTIFIC LAWS

There are similarities between laws and principles that describe economics or social phenomena and scientific laws and theories. A few of them are:

1. The Ideal Gas Law

$$PV = nRT$$

Represents the ideal gas law, which relates pressure (P), volume (V), molecules of gas (n), a constant (R) and temperature (T). If we also hold n constant, it may be rewritten as:

$$\frac{P \; \alpha \; T}{V}$$

For a given amount of gas, pressure is directly proportional to temperature (as temperature increases, pressure increases). Pressure is inversely proportional to Volume (increasing volume decreases the pressure). In economics, as demand increases at constant supply, the price increases (directly proportional). As supply increases at constant demand, the price decreases (inversely proportional). Wage and price controls in an economy have the same effect as turning off the pressure sensor on a boiler. The unseen price, determined by economic law, will result in shortages.

2. Action and Reaction

For every action, there is an equal and opposite reaction.

The above principle of physics also applies to social and economic behavior, with a few subtle modifications. In the latter cases, the reaction is not always immediate, equal, or exactly in the opposite direction. For example, when a new tax law is passed, lawyers and accountants begin to look for loopholes or creative work-arounds.

3. The Principle of Inertia

An object at rest tends to stay at rest; an object in motion, tends to stay in motion.

Anyone who has slid a box across a floor is familiar with inertia. It requires more force to get it started, than it does to keep it moving. It takes less energy to move the box all the way, than it does to stop and start. Business processes, particularly in manufacturing, tend to be more efficient when they are continuous, than when they are stop and go.

4. Conservation of Momentum

Momentum is defined as the product of mass and velocity (mxv). A large object, like a train, has much greater momentum than a smaller object like an automobile, traveling at the same speed. It takes much more effort to stop or change the direction of a large object. Similarly, it takes much more effort to change the behavior of a large corporation than it does for a family-owned business.

217

Thank You for Reading Compassionate Capitalism

Please post a review on Amazon.com

And

Look for other great books by Gerard Hansen

Artemis Conspiracy

www.ingramcontent.com/pod-product-compliance
Lightning Source LLC
Chambersburg PA
CBHW020751300326
41914CB00050B/122